A Note From Rick Renner

I am on a personal quest to see a "revival of the Bible" so people can establish their lives on a firm foundation that will stand strong and endure the test when the end-time storm winds begin to intensify.

In order to experience a revival of the Bible in your personal life, it is important to take time each day to read, receive, and apply its truths to your life. James tells us that if we will continue in the perfect law of liberty — refusing to be forgetful hearers but determined to be doers — we will be blessed in our ways. As you watch or listen to the programs in this series and work through this corresponding study guide, I trust that you will search the Scriptures and allow the Holy Spirit to help you hear something new from God's Word that applies specifically to your life. I encourage you to be a doer of the Word that He reveals to you. Whatever the cost, I assure you — it will be worth it.

> Thy words were found, and I did eat them;
> and thy word was unto me the joy and rejoicing of mine heart:
> for I am called by thy name, O Lord God of hosts.
> —Jeremiah 15:16

Your brother and friend in Jesus Christ,

Rick Renner

Unless otherwise indicated, all scripture quotations are taken from the *King James Version* of the Bible.

Scripture quotations marked (*AMPC*) are taken from the *Amplified® Bible*. Copyright © 1954, 1958, 1962, 1964, 1965, 1987 by The Lockman Foundation. Used by permission. **www.Lockman.org**.

Scripture quotations marked (*NKJV*) are taken from the *New King James Version®*. Copyright © 1982 by Thomas Nelson. Used by permission. All rights reserved.

God's Hall of Faith

Copyright © 2020 by Rick Renner
8316 E. 73rd St.
Tulsa, Oklahoma 74133

Published by Rick Renner Ministries
www.renner.org

ISBN 13: 978-1-68031-812-8

eBook ISBN 13: 978-1-68031-813-5

All rights reserved. No portion of this book may be reproduced or transmitted in any form or by any means — electronic, mechanical, photocopy, recording, scanning, or other — except for brief quotations in critical reviews or articles, without the prior written permission of the Publisher.

How To Use This Study Guide

This ten-lesson study guide corresponds to *"God's Hall of Faith" With Rick Renner* (Renner TV). Each lesson in this study guide covers a topic that is addressed during the program series, with questions and references supplied to draw you deeper into your own private study of the Scriptures on this subject.

To derive the most benefit from this study guide, consider the following:

First, watch or listen to the program prior to working through the corresponding lesson in this guide. (Programs can also be viewed at **renner.org** by clicking on the Media/Archives links.)

Second, take the time to look up the scriptures included in each lesson. Prayerfully consider their application to your own life.

Third, use a journal or notebook to make note of your answers to each lesson's Study Questions and Practical Application challenges.

Fourth, invest specific time in prayer and in the Word of God to consult with the Holy Spirit. Write down the scriptures or insights He reveals to you.

Finally, take action! Whatever the Lord tells you to do according to His Word, do it.

For added insights on this subject, it is recommended that you obtain Rick Renner's books *Sparkling Gems From the Greek, Volumes 1* and *2*. You may also select from Rick's other available resources by placing your order at **renner.org** or by calling 1-800-742-5593.

LESSON 1

TOPIC

Do Not Cast Away Your Confession of Faith

SCRIPTURES

1. **Hebrews 10:35-39** — Cast not away therefore your confidence, which hath great recompence of reward. For ye have need of patience, that, after ye have done the will of God, ye might receive the promise. For yet a little while, and he that shall come will come, and will not tarry. Now the just shall live by faith: but if any man draw back, my soul shall have no pleasure in him. But we are not of them who draw back unto perdition; but of them that believe to the saving of the soul.
2. **Hebrews 11:1-3** — Now faith is the substance of things hoped for, the evidence of things not seen. For by it the elders obtained a good report. Through faith we understand that the worlds were framed by the word of God, so that things which are seen were not made of things which do appear.

GREEK WORDS

1. "cast" — ἀποβάλλω (*apoballo*): to throw away; to discard; or to get rid of something no longer desired, needed, or wanted
2. "confidence" — παρρησία (*parresia*): a bold, frank, forthright speech; confidence; audacious; emboldened; openness; extraordinarily frank; a daring to speak what one believes or thinks, possibly even in the face of retribution; boldness; assurance; unashamed confidence; it is a frankness of speech that accompanies unflinching authority
3. "recompense of reward" — μισθαποδοσία (*misthapodosia*): the word for money, salary, or a payment that is due; primarily used to denote a payment, salary, or reward given for a job performed; can describe a recompense, reimbursement, settlement, or reparation; being reimbursed for an expense a person has paid out of his own pocket in order to get his job done; a full and complete recompense

4. "patience" — ὑπομονή (*hupomone*): to stay or to abide; to remain in one's spot; to keep a position; to resolve to maintain territory that has been gained; in a military sense to picture soldiers who were ordered to maintain their positions even in the face of fierce combat; to defiantly stick it out regardless of the pressure mounted against it; endurance; staying power; hang-in-there power; the attitude that holds out, holds on, outlasts, perseveres, and hangs in there, never giving up, refusing to surrender to obstacles, and turning down every opportunity to quit; it pictures one who is under a heavy load but refuses to bend, break, or surrender because he is convinced that the territory, promise, or principle under assault rightfully belongs to him; stamina, durability

5. "receive" — κομίζω (*komidzo*): receive; to convey to someone else; to receive what is due; to receive what one has coming to him

6. "draw back" — ὑποστέλλω (*hupostello*): to shrink back; one who is withdrawing, retreating, regressing, receding, backing away, backsliding, or recoiling from something; one who reverses his direction; to move backward instead of forward; to back off and retreat from an object, principle, or task

7. "perdition" — ἀπώλεια (*apoleia*): something ruined, rotten, and decomposing; used to describe the stench of a decaying animal or a dead human body; a loathsome, putrid, vulgar, disgusting, nauseating scent; something in the process of perishing; doomed, rotten, ruinous, or decaying

8. "now" — δὲ (*de*): but; on the other hand

9. "faith" — πίστις (*pistis*): its root means to persuade, to trust, to believe; a persuasion from God that imparts an impulse or "divine spark" to believe; hence, faith; in secular antiquity referred to a guarantee or warranty of something that was sure; a force that is propelled forward toward a goal

10. "substance" — ὑπόστασις (*hupostasis*): a compound of ὑπό (*hupo*) and ἵστημι (*histimi*); the word ὑπό (*hupo*) means by or under, and the word ἵστημι (*histimi*) means to stand; literally, to stand by something; the attitude and actions of one who has determined to stand by something promised and refuses to budge from it; a fixed decision that one will be unmoving and he will stay or stand by a person, principle, promise, or territory

11. "hoped for" — ἐλπίζω (*elpidzo*): to actively hope for the fulfillment of something expected; the form used in this verse is continuous, being hoped for, stressing that the manifestation has not come yet
12. "evidence" — ἔλεγχος (*elegchos*): to expose, convict, or cross-examine for the purpose of conviction, as when convicting a lawbreaker in a court of law; the image of a lawyer who brings forth evidence that is indisputable and undeniable, so that the accused person's actions are irrefutably brought to light and as a result the offender is exposed and convicted; also used positively to convince someone of something; used to denote a lawyer who worked diligently to convince people of a new way of thinking or a new way of seeing things; in this case, they weren't trying to convict someone, they were working to convince someone
13. "elders" — πρεσβύτεροι (*presbuteroi*): elders; the respected ones; in this case, heroes of faith
14. "we understand" — νοοῦμεν (*nooumen*): plural form of νοέω (*noeo*), to think or to understand; indicates intelligent activity; we think, we conclude, we rationalize, we understand
15. "worlds" — αἰῶνας (*aionas*): from αἰών (*aion*), an age or era; a specific time, age, or era within the past history of mankind; different periods of time
16. "framed" — καταρτίζω (*katartidzo*): to change, to mend, to adjust, or to alter the form or shape of an already existing thing; re-creating, reshaping, remolding, and altering something that is already in existence; not so much the act of creation, but the act of transformation
17. "the word of God" — ῥήματι Θεοῦ (*rhemati Theou*): by a word from God

SYNOPSIS

The ten lessons in this study on ***God's Hall of Faith*** will focus on the following topics:

- Do Not Cast Away Your Confession of Faith
- Standing By a Word From God
- Enoch: Believing for a Personal Rapture
- Noah: The Man Who Refused To Give Up
- Abraham: The Father of Faith

- Sarah: A Woman Who Counted God Faithful
- Isaac, Jacob, Joseph: Believing for the Next Generation
- Moses: A Man With an Assignment
- Gideon, Barak, Sampson, Jepthae, David, Samuel, and Others
- Unnamed Giants of Faith

The emphasis of this lesson:
God warns us not to cast away our confidence in Him or His promises. He wants us to hold tightly to our faith, allowing His supernatural patience to develop in us. Payday is coming! And we will receive the full recompense and reward if we don't draw back.

Located in Saint Petersburg, Russia is the legendary Winter Palace. It is the massive residence where the Romanov family spent their winters and ruled the Russian Empire. In 1754, the order to build the palace was issued by Empress Elizabeth — who was known as "the party queen" because she loved balls and festivities. Sadly, she died in 1761 just before it was completed. Upon her death, Peter III took the throne; he was the grandson of Peter the Great and was married to a young German girl named Catherine II.

History reveals that Catherine didn't like her husband, so she had him overthrown and assumed rule of the nation as the Empress of Russia. Catherine II became known as Catherine the Great, and she was the first to move into the Winter Palace in 1762. As the tsarina of Russia, she governed from the Winter Palace, ruling about one-sixth of the earth's surface. That was the extent of the Russian Empire at that time.

What is amazing about the Winter Palace — and the adjoining Hermitage Palace which was added on years later — is its enormous size. The combined square footage of these fortresses is 2,511,000 square feet. That is the equivalent of about 3 football fields. But when you factor in the second and third floors and the basement, the area is equal to about 12 football fields! Just the hallways alone, if placed end to end, would measure 15 miles!

The Winter Palace is a hall of history where great leaders from the past are commemorated. Every single room tells a story about a different leader in Russia's history. In a similar way, the Bible has a hall of history. Actually, we call it "God's Hall of Faith," and it is found in Hebrews 11. This is where God commemorates many of the great men and women of Old Testament Scripture who accomplished great feats through unbendable, unbreakable faith.

Cast Not Away Your Confidence

Just before talking about the great heroes of the faith, the writer of Hebrews took time to encourage a group of believers who were really struggling in their faith not to give up. It appears they had been believing for God to answer their prayers for a very long time, but they hadn't seen any results. Thus, he said, "Cast not away therefore your confidence, which hath great recompence of reward" (Hebrews 10:35).

The word "cast" here is a translation of the Greek word *apoballo*, which is a compound of the word *apo*, meaning *away*, and the word *ballo*, meaning *to throw*. When these words are combined to form the word *apoballo*, it means *to throw away*; *to discard*; or *to get rid of something no longer desired, needed, or wanted*. This same word *apoballo* is used in Mark 10:50, where blind Bartimaeus was trying to get to Jesus. The verse says, "And he, casting away his garment, rose, and came to Jesus." The phrase "casting away" is *apoballo*. Hindered by the garment wrapped around him, Bartimaeus ripped it off and threw it aside in order to get to Jesus to receive his healing.

The writer of Hebrews used the word *apoballo* — translated as "cast not away" — to urge believers not to throw away or discard their confidence. After waiting and waiting for God to answer their prayers, they had become quite weary and were tempted to get rid of their confession of faith. The struggle to keep believing and trusting God was very real. It's possible they were thinking, *What is the use to keep believing? If God was going to do something, surely He would have done it by now. Our faith is just a hindrance that is keeping us from getting where we want to be.*

"Cast not away therefore your confidence..." the writer pleaded (Hebrews 10:35). The word "confidence" is a translation of the Greek word *parresia*, and it describes *a bold, frank, forthright kind of speech*. It depicts *confidence; one that is audacious or emboldened*. It denotes *openness* and carries the idea of being *extraordinarily frank*. It is *daring to speak what one believes or thinks without hesitation — possibly even in the face of retribution*. Furthermore, it means *boldness*; *assurance*; *unashamed confidence*; *it is a frankness of speech that accompanies unflinching authority*.

The use of the word *parresia* — translated here as "confidence" — tells us that the Hebrew believers being addressed were very bold and audacious in their confession of faith when they began their walk with God. But because the answers to their prayers hadn't come yet, they were tempted to throw it all away as though the manifestation was never going to come to pass.

'Patience' Is Needed To Receive God's Promises

What was the reason for not casting away their confidence? The Bible says that maintaining confidence "…hath great recompence of reward" (Hebrews 10:35). The phrase "recompense of reward" is from the Greek word *misthapodosia*, which is the term for *money, salary, or a payment that is due*. It is primarily used to denote *a payment, salary, or reward given for a job performed*. It can also describe *a recompense, reimbursement, settlement, or reparation*. It means *to be reimbursed for an expense a person has paid out of his own pocket in order to get his job done*; *a full and complete recompense*.

Here the writer of Hebrews basically said, "If you will hang on and continue to boldly confess your faith in God, payday is coming! He is going to reimburse you for everything you've given out." Then he adds in the next verse, "For ye have need of patience, that, after ye have done the will of God, ye might receive the promise" (Hebrews 10:36).

Although this may have been the last thing this group of believers wanted to hear, it was what they needed to hear. The word "patience" is the Greek word *hupomone*, and it is packed with profound meaning. It is a compound of the word *hupo*, meaning *under*, and the word *meno*, meaning *to stay* or *to abide*. When these words are joined to form the word *hupomone*, it means *to stay or to abide*; *to remain in one's spot*, or *to keep a position*. It indicates *a resolve to maintain territory that has been gained*. It is to be *immovable* until the thing prayed for is manifested. In a military sense, it pictures soldiers who were ordered to maintain their positions even in the face of fierce combat.

Moreover, the word "patience" — *hupomone* — means *to defiantly stick it out regardless of the pressure mounted against it*. It embodies the idea of *endurance*; *staying power*; or *hang-in-there power*. It is *the attitude that holds out, holds on, outlasts, perseveres, and hangs in there, never giving up, refusing to surrender to obstacles, and turning down every opportunity to quit*.

It pictures one who is under a heavy load but refuses to bend, break, or surrender because he is convinced that the territory, promise, or principle under assault rightfully belongs to him. This person is thoroughly committed to maintaining his position and staying in his spot as long as it's necessary for him to achieve victory. The word *hupomone* can also describe *stamina* or *durability*.

The writer of Hebrews said, "For ye have need of patience, that, after ye have done the will of God, ye might receive the promise" (Hebrews 10:36). The word "receive" is also important. In Greek, it is the word *komidzo*, which literally means *to receive what is due* or *to receive what one has coming to him*. The inclusion of this word in this passage is the equivalent of saying, "Whatever promise of God you have been declaring by faith — whatever you have been boldly speaking and believing God for — is coming to you. It is your *recompense* or *reward* that is on its way to you — as long as you don't give up."

What Does It Mean To 'Draw Back' From Faith?

In Hebrews 10:37, the Bible goes on to say, "For yet a little while, and he that shall come will come, and will not tarry." The word "little" in this verse is the Greek word *micros*, and it describes *something that is microscopic*. Here the Holy Spirit is encouraging us by letting us know that in a *microscopic* amount of time, the answer we have been waiting for will come. In other words, *payday is on its way…* as long as we — *hupomone* — hang in there, stay put, and don't quit.

When we come to verse 38, the writer makes this declaration: "Now the just shall live by faith: but if any man draw back, my soul shall have no pleasure in him." Notice the phrase "draw back." It is the Greek word *hupostello*, which means *to shrink back*. It pictures *one who is withdrawing, retreating, regressing, receding, backing away, backsliding, or recoiling from something*. This shrinking back usually takes place gradually, one step at a time. As this person experiences one little discouragement after another, he releases his grip on his confession of faith. Furthermore, the word *hupostello* depicts *one who reverses his direction*. It carries the idea of *moving backward instead of forward*. It means *to back off and retreat from an object, principle, or task*.

That is what the Hebrew believers were tempted to do. They were thinking things like, *Why should we keep believing and standing in faith? Surely what we're believing for should have happened by now. Our lives have been on hold. We could have moved on, but no! We had to have a word from God and make a declaration of faith. Ever since then, we've been stuck here believing and confessing, believing and confessing. Maybe we should just abandon all of this and move on.*

But the writer of Hebrews immediately responded in the next verse by saying, "But we are not of them who draw back unto perdition; but of them that believe to the saving of the soul" (Hebrews 10:39). Once again we see the phrase "draw back" — the Greek word *hupostello*. In this case, he is saying, "We are *not* the kind of people that *shrink back, withdraw*, or *retreat* from our position of faith." Specifically he said, "But we are not of them who draw back unto perdition…" (Hebrews 10:39).

The Reason Why Some People's Lives 'Stink'

The word "perdition" is the Greek word *apoleia*, and it pictures *something ruined, rotten, and decomposing*. It was used to describe *the stench of a decaying animal or a dead human body*. It denoted *a loathsome, putrid, vulgar, disgusting, nauseating scent; something in the process of perishing; something doomed, rotten, ruinous, or decaying*. This word *apoleia* — translated here as "perdition" — gives us a vivid picture of what happens to people who retreat from their position of faith. When they throw away their faith, they begin to emit a terrible spiritual stench and acquire a nauseating attitude of cynicism and bitterness about life and those who are walking in faith. If you've ever been there, you know how awful this condition can be.

That is why the writer of Hebrews urged his readers — both then and now — to live by *faith*. This word "faith" in Hebrews 10:38 is the Greek word *pistis*, and it describes *a force that is propelling one forward toward a goal*. Its root means *to persuade, to trust*, or *to believe*. It is *a persuasion from God that imparts an impulse or "divine spark" to believe*; hence, *faith*. When you're in faith, you are moving forward. But when you release or walk away from your faith, you are moving in reverse — you are losing territory and drifting into negativity.

Friend, hold tightly to your faith and continue to boldly declare the promises God has made to you. Payday is coming! In that moment, you will receive the answer to your prayers. Relationships will be restored, deliverance will occur, financial provision will be received, and healing will take place.

In our next lesson, we will begin examining "God's Hall of Faith" in Hebrews 11 and see how ordinary people received a word from God and began declaring it with confidence. Although they had opportunities to throw away their faith and walk away, they refused to do so. Consequently, they obtained a good report and effectively changed history.

STUDY QUESTIONS

> Study to shew thyself approved unto God, a workman that needeth not to be ashamed, rightly dividing the word of truth.
> — 2 Timothy 2:15

1. According to Romans 12:3 and Ephesians 2:8 and 9, where does faith come from and who has it?
2. Hebrews 10:36 says, "For ye have need of patience, that, after ye have done the will of God, ye might receive the promise." How are Galatians 6:9 and James 1:12 very similar to this passage in Hebrews? (Also consider Revelation 3:11.)

PRACTICAL APPLICATION

> But be ye doers of the word, and not hearers only, deceiving your own selves.
> — James 1:22

1. The believers the writer addressed in Hebrews had been waiting and waiting for God to answer their prayers, but they still had not seen any results. Are you in a similar situation? What have you been praying for God to do in your life for a long time that has still not come to pass?
2. The Bible says those who "draw back" from faith are those who *withdraw*, *retreat* or *backslide* unto "perdition," which means they begin to emit a terrible spiritual stench and develop a nauseating attitude of cynicism and bitterness. Have you or someone you know experienced these symptoms? If so, how would you describe the condition of your/their life and family?
3. Be honest: Have you *drawn back* from your faith in God in a particular area? Are you disappointed or offended with Him over something? If so, explain your situation? What has caused you to spiritually retreat and reverse your direction? Take a few moments to pour out

your heart to God, asking Him to forgive you of anything specific He brings to mind.

LESSON 2

TOPIC
Standing By a Word From God

SCRIPTURES
1. **Hebrews 10:35-39** — Cast not away therefore your confidence, which hath great recompence of reward. For ye have need of patience, that, after ye have done the will of God, ye might receive the promise. For yet a little while, and he that shall come will come, and will not tarry. Now the just shall live by faith: but if any man draw back, my soul shall have no pleasure in him. But we are not of them who draw back unto perdition; but of them that believe to the saving of the soul.
2. **Hebrews 11:1-3** — Now faith is the substance of things hoped for, the evidence of things not seen. For by it the elders obtained a good report. Through faith we understand that the worlds were framed by the word of God, so that things which are seen were not made of things which do appear.

GREEK WORDS
1. "cast" — **ἀποβάλλω** (*apoballo*): to throw away; to discard; or to get rid of something no longer desired, needed, or wanted
2. "confidence" — **παρρησία** (*parresia*): a bold, frank, forthright speech; confidence; audacious; emboldened; openness; extraordinarily frank; a daring to speak what one believes or thinks, possibly even in the face of retribution; boldness; assurance; unashamed confidence; it is a frankness of speech that accompanies unflinching authority
3. "recompense of reward" — **μισθαποδοσία** (*misthapodosia*): the word for money, salary, or a payment that is due; primarily used to denote a payment, salary, or reward given for a job performed; can describe a recompense, reimbursement, settlement, or reparation; being reimbursed for an expense a person has paid out of his own pocket in order to get his job done; a full and complete recompense

4. "patience" — ὑπομονή (*hupomone*): to stay or to abide; to remain in one's spot; to keep a position; to resolve to maintain territory that has been gained; in a military sense to picture soldiers who were ordered to maintain their positions even in the face of fierce combat; to defiantly stick it out regardless of the pressure mounted against it; endurance; staying power; hang-in-there power; the attitude that holds out, holds on, outlasts, perseveres, and hangs in there, never giving up, refusing to surrender to obstacles, and turning down every opportunity to quit; it pictures one who is under a heavy load but refuses to bend, break, or surrender because he is convinced that the territory, promise, or principle under assault rightfully belongs to him; stamina, durability

5. "receive" — κομίζω (*komidzo*): receive; to convey to someone else; to receive what is due; to receive what one has coming to him

6. "draw back" — ὑποστέλλω (*hupostello*): to shrink back; one who is withdrawing, retreating, regressing, receding, backing away, backsliding, or recoiling from something; one who reverses his direction; to move backward instead of forward; to back off and retreat from an object, principle, or task

7. "perdition" — ἀπώλεια (*apoleia*): something ruined, rotten, and decomposing; used to describe the stench of a decaying animal or a dead human body; a loathsome, putrid, vulgar, disgusting, nauseating scent; something in the process of perishing; doomed, rotten, ruinous, or decaying

8. "now" — δὲ (*de*): but; on the other hand

9. "faith" — πίστις (*pistis*): its root means to persuade, to trust, to believe; a persuasion from God that imparts an impulse or "divine spark" to believe; hence, faith; in secular antiquity referred to a guarantee or warranty of something that was sure; a force that is propelled forward toward a goal

10. "substance" — ὑπόστασις (*hupostasis*): a compound of ὑπό (*hupo*) and ἵστημι (*histimi*); the word ὑπό (*hupo*) means by or under, and the word ἵστημι (*histimi*) means to stand; literally, to stand by something; the attitude and actions of one who has determined to stand by something promised and refuses to budge from it; a fixed decision that one will be unmoving and he will stay or stand by a person, principle, promise, or territory

11. "hoped for" — ἐλπίζω (*elpidzo*): to actively hope for the fulfillment of something expected; the form used in this verse is continuous, being hoped for, stressing that the manifestation has not come yet
12. "evidence" — ἔλεγχος (*elegchos*): to expose, convict, or cross-examine for the purpose of conviction, as when convicting a lawbreaker in a court of law; the image of a lawyer who brings forth evidence that is indisputable and undeniable, so that the accused person's actions are irrefutably brought to light and as a result the offender is exposed and convicted; also used positively to convince someone of something; used to denote a lawyer who worked diligently to convince people of a new way of thinking or a new way of seeing things; in this case, they weren't trying to convict someone, they were working to convince someone
13. "elders" — πρεσβύτεροι (*presbuteroi*): elders; the respected ones; in this case, heroes of faith
14. "we understand" — νοοῦμεν (*nooumen*): plural form of νοέω (*noeo*), to think or to understand; indicates intelligent activity; we think, we conclude, we rationalize, we understand
15. "worlds" — αἰῶνας (*aionas*): from αἰών (*aion*), an age or era; a specific time, age, or era within the past history of mankind; different periods of time
16. "framed" — καταρτίζω (*katartidzo*): to change, to mend, to adjust, or to alter the form or shape of an already existing thing; re-creating, reshaping, remolding, and altering something that is already in existence; not so much the act of creation, but the act of transformation
17. "the word of God" — ῥήματι Θεοῦ (*rhemati Theou*): by a word from God

SYNOPSIS

The Winter Palace, which is located in Saint Petersburg, Russia, was first occupied by Catherine the Great in 1762. But after her, it was the winter residence of the Romanov family until 1917. The Romanovs were rulers of Russia, presiding over the largest empire in world history. It covered one-sixth of the surface of the earth, and the Winter Palace was one of their major headquarters.

As we learned in Lesson 1, the Winter Palace was an enormous fortress where the Romanov family welcomed ambassadors, kings, and queens from all around the world. They held fabulous balls and banquets, accommodating 2,000 people at just one table who were served by 4,000 servants! It was not uncommon for attendees to partake of as many as 500 courses of food in a single banquet. Indeed, the Winter Palace was a place of unrivaled opulence and luxury until 1917 when the Bolshevik Revolution took place.

When dignitaries from Europe came to Russia to visit the tsar and his family, they arrived by ship via the Neva River. As they entered the Winter Palace, they were first escorted into the Jordan Gallery, which was filled with remarkable sculptures from the Greek and Roman world. Guests were then taken up the extravagant Jordan Staircase, which was massive in size and featured magnificent columns, exquisite ceiling paintings, and was decorated with more than 11 pounds of gold. The purpose for all this magnificence was to impress the arriving guests and make them feel very small. Even those who had come from the great palaces of Europe had never seen anything like it.

Visitors were then guided through the Field Marshal Room, the commemoration room of Peter the Great, the colossal room of the coat of arms, and the 1812 Gallery. From there they would be ushered into the Great Throne Room where they would meet and greet the tsar or tsarina. For Russians, there was no greater place where past heroes were honored and celebrated.

For Old Testament believers, Hebrews 11 is a place of great honor. It's what we call "God's Hall of Faith." People like Enoch, Noah, Abraham, and Sarah are all celebrated as heroes for their great faith. They each received a word from God and held on to it tightly until it came to pass and they received what they were believing for. Friend, there's room in God's Hall of Faith for you, and He wants you to be in it!

The emphasis of this lesson:

Faith relentlessly stands by God's promises. It actively hopes and is strongly convinced that it has what it cannot see. The Old Testament heroes of faith displayed this kind of faith. They received a word from God, faithfully stood by it, and transformed their generations.

In our first lesson, we saw how the writer of Hebrews wrote to believers who had been standing in faith for a long time, believing for God to come through, but they had become exhausted from waiting. In fact, they were so weary that they were thinking about walking away from the faith. That is why the writer wrote and urged them, "Cast not away therefore your confidence, which hath great recompence of reward" (Hebrews 10:35). Basically, he told them, "Payday is coming! What you have been believing and waiting for is on its way! Just don't throw away your bold confession of faith and miss out on God's reimbursement."

What Is Faith?

In the eleventh chapter of Hebrews, the writer makes a statement that has become one of the greatest power passages of Christianity since the First Century. He said, "Now faith is the substance of things hoped for, the evidence of things not seen" (Hebrews 11:1). For many believers, this verse has been rather abstract and difficult to understand. But a careful reading of this passage in the Greek New Testament reveals this verse in a whole new light.

For instance, in the original Greek, the word "now" does not appear. It actually starts out with the Greek word *de*, which is a comparative word meaning *but* or *on the other hand*. Hence, the opening of the verse would better be translated as, "*But* faith is the substance of things hoped for," or "*On the other hand*, faith is the substance of things hoped for...."

Remember, the writer of Hebrews just wrapped up chapter 10 encouraging his readers to hold tightly to their confession of faith and not draw back into spiritual ruin and decay. In chapter 11, he shifts his focus to talk about individuals who held on to their faith and effectively changed history as a result.

"So what is faith?" you ask. Good question! The word "faith" is the Greek word *pistis*, which is a well-known word used throughout the New Testament. It comes from a root that means *to persuade, to trust, or to believe*. It describes *a supernatural persuasion from God that imparts an impulse or "divine spark" to believe*, which means faith is a gift from God. He is the One who gives us the divine ability to believe; it is not something we conjure up on our own. In secular antiquity, the word *pistis* referred to *a guarantee or warranty of something that was sure*. It also signified *a force that propels one forward toward a goal*.

To be clear, faith is never in retreat — never. It is a divine force that always propels one forward. If you are in retreat, you are not in faith.

Faith Stands By God's Promises

The Bible says, "Now faith is the substance of things hoped for…" (Hebrews 11:1). The word "substance" has certainly caused many to scratch their heads in wonder, but in Greek its meaning is quite clear. It is the word *hupostasis*, which is a compound of the words *hupo* and *histimi*. The word *hupo* means *by*, and the word *histimi* means *to stand*. When these two words are compounded to form *hupostasis*, it literally means *to stand by something*. It is *the attitude and actions of one who has determined to stand by something promised and refuses to budge from it*. It denotes *a fixed decision that one will be unmoving and he will stay or stand by a person, principle, promise, or territory*.

If you think about it, the word "substance" is more a description of how faith *behaves* rather than a definition of what it is. Again, the writer is comparing what a withdrawal from faith looks like at the end of Hebrews 10 with how faith behaves in Hebrews 11. If we insert the meaning of the words "faith" and "substance" into Hebrews 11:1, it says, "Now faith — *the supernatural persuasion from God that imparts an impulse or "divine spark" to believe* — is the substance of things hoped for — it *stands by unmoved, refusing to budge from what God has promised.*"

In many ways, faith behaves like a bulldog that has found the bone of its wildest dreams. Driven by insatiable desire, that dog tenaciously wraps its jaws around that bone as if its life depended on it. No matter how hard you tug or try to pull that bone away, that dog has decided it's going to stand by its bone and never let it go. That is the idea being communicated through the word "substance."

Friend, if you have been standing by God's promises for healing, don't let go of them. Likewise, if you have been believing and standing by His words for financial provision or the restoration of your relationships, hold tightly to His truth. Whatever you're believing God to do in your marriage, your family, your business, your church, or your community, continue to tenaciously hold tightly to His promises. Like a bulldog grasping his bone, never let them go.

Faith Actively Hopes and Is Strongly Convinced of Things Not Seen

The Bible says we are to stand by and hold tightly to "…things hoped for…" (Hebrews 11:1). The phrase "hoped for" is a translation of the Greek word *elpidzo*, which means *to actively hope for the fulfillment of something expected*. Although it has not happened yet, there is an active expectation that it will take place. The form of the word *elpidzo* here is *continuous*. Hence, it is something being hoped for, stressing that the manifestation has not come yet. Again, this is more of a description of how faith behaves rather than a definition.

How else does the Bible describe faith? Hebrews 11:1 says it is "…the evidence of things not seen." The word "evidence" is the Greek word *elegchos*, which was a term regularly used in a court of law. It means *to expose, convict, or cross-examine for the purpose of conviction, as when convicting a lawbreaker in a court of law*. It is the image of a lawyer who brings forth evidence that is indisputable and undeniable, so that the accused person's actions are irrefutably brought to light and as a result the offender is exposed and convicted.

In contrast, the word *elegchos* can also be used positively *to convince someone of something*. In this verse, it is used to denote *a lawyer who worked diligently to convince people of a new way of thinking or a new way of seeing things*. In this case, they weren't trying to convict someone of a crime; they were working to convince someone of something positive. Thus, when you are in faith, you have a very strong conviction that what God has promised is undoubtedly going to happen.

So taking the original Greek meaning of the words in Hebrews 11:1, we see that…

- FAITH is a "divine spark" from God to believe; a force that propels us forward toward a goal.
- FAITH stands by and never lets go of what it is believing God for.
- FAITH is a very strong conviction that what God has promised is going to happen.

Please realize that when you are in faith, pressure to abandon God's promises and walk away from your confession of faith *will* come. The people listed in God's Hall of Faith in Hebrews 11 experienced great pressures, but they were convinced in their hearts that what God had spoken to them would come to pass. Therefore, they persistently stood by God's word to them and saw His promises come to pass. That is what Hebrews 11:2 tells us: "For by it [faith] the elders obtained a good report."

The Heroes of the Old Testament Transformed Their Generation

When we come to Hebrews 11:3, it says, "Through faith we understand that the worlds were framed by the word of God, so that things which are seen were not made of things which do appear." Although it may seem as though the writer has switched gears and has started talking about the days of creation, a closer look at the meaning of the original Greek reveals otherwise.

First of all, we must take into consideration the context of Hebrews 11:2 in order to understand Hebrews 11:3. In verse 2, the writer mentions the "elders" who obtained a good report by their unbendable, unbreakable, never-give-up faith. The word "elders" is the Greek word *presbuteroi*, and it describes the *elders* or the *respected ones*. In this case, it refers to *the heroes of faith in the Old Testament*.

The Old Testament heroes being talked about in Hebrews 11:2 are the same ones being talked about in Hebrews 11:3. It says, "Through faith we understand that the worlds were framed by the word of God...." The word "faith" in this verse is again the Greek word *pistis*, and it describes *the unflinching, immovable, never-give-up trust and belief in what God has said*.

The phrase "we understand" is a translation of the Greek word *nooumen*, which is the plural form of the word *noeo*, meaning *to think* or *to understand*. This word indicates *intelligent activity* and could be translated as *we think, we conclude, we rationalize*, or *we understand*.

This brings us to the phrase "the worlds were framed." Here, the word "worlds" is not the Greek word *ges*, which describes the *planet*, or the Greek word *cosmos*, which describes the *universe*. Instead, the word "worlds" in verse 3 is the Greek word *aionas*, which is from the word *aion*, and it describes *an age* or *era*. It is *a specific time, age, or era within the past history of mankind; different periods of time*. The word *aionas* would never be used to describe creation.

Next is the word "framed" — the Greek word *katartidzo*, which means *to change, to mend, to adjust, or to alter the form or shape of an already existing thing*. Hence, it indicates *re-creating, reshaping, remolding, and the altering of something that is already in existence*. It is not so much the act of creation, but the act of transformation. Then there is the phrase "the word of God." In Greek, these words are actually *by a word from God*.

Taking the Greek meaning of these key words, Hebrews 11:3 would better be translated:

"Through faith — through the unbendable, unbreakable, never-give-up kind of faith that stands by what it's hoping for in God's Word — we understand that the different time periods within the past history of mankind (different generations, decades, centuries, and millennia) have been framed — altered, modified, and radically changed — by individuals who received a word from God, so that things which are seen were not made of things which do appear."

Again, if we remain true to the context of Hebrews chapters 10 and 11, Hebrews 11:3 is talking about individuals in the Old Testament who received a word from God, and through their faith — their decision to tenaciously stand by and hold on to what God promised — they changed the history of their generation and the world.

Think about it. Noah, Abraham, Sarah, and Gideon were ordinary people who each received a word from God. And because they faithfully stood by that word, they adjusted, amended, and changed their generations and left the world better than they found it.

Friend, that is the dynamic power of receiving and believing a word from God! That is why the devil is fighting so hard to get you to cast away your confidence and give up. He knows that if you will stand by the word God has given you, you will change your generation. You will transform your family, your business, your church, and the world in which you live.

In our next lesson, we turn our attention to a man named Enoch who received a word from God and gave us an example of what the rapture of the Church will be like.

STUDY QUESTIONS

> Study to shew thyself approved unto God, a workman that needeth
> not to be ashamed, rightly dividing the word of truth.
> — 2 Timothy 2:15

1. The Bible says that *faith* — which is the ability to believe and trust God and His Word — is a gift from God. According to Romans 10:17, what should you do regularly to get your faith to grow? (Also consider Luke 8:15; John 8:31,32; James 1:21.)
2. What specifically are you believing God to do in your *marriage*, your *family*, your *business*, your *church*, or your *community*? What related scriptures are you holding on to and confessing out loud in faith?

PRACTICAL APPLICATION

> But be ye doers of the word, and not hearers only,
> deceiving your own selves.
> —James 1:22

1. Prior to this lesson, what did you understand *faith* to be? How has your understanding been changed by this teaching?
2. In your own words, briefly describe how faith behaves. Which of these attributes can you see at work in your own life?
3. Looking back at the lives of your parents, grandparents, and extended family, who can you see in your family line that faithfully stood by God's Word? How did their actions affect the people around them? What verse or passages were they holding on to? How has their faith impacted your life?

LESSON 3

TOPIC
Enoch: Believing for a Personal Rapture

SCRIPTURES
1. **Hebrews 10:35,39** — Cast not away therefore your confidence, which hath great recompence of reward. …But we are not of them who draw back unto perdition; but of them that believe to the saving of the soul.
2. **Hebrews 11:1-3,5** — Now faith is the substance of things hoped for, the evidence of things not seen. For by it the elders obtained a good report. Through faith we understand that the worlds were framed by the word of God, so that things which are seen were not made of things which do appear. …By faith Enoch was translated that he should not see death; and was not found, because God had translated him: for before his translation he had this testimony, that he pleased God.
3. **Jude 14** — And Enoch also, the seventh from Adam, prophesied of these, saying, Behold, the Lord cometh with ten thousands of his saints.
4. **Genesis 5:21-24** — And Enoch lived sixty and five years, and begat Methuselah: And Enoch walked with God after he begat Methuselah three hundred years, and begat sons and daughters: And all the days of Enoch were three hundred sixty and five years: And Enoch walked with God: and he was not; for God took him.

GREEK WORDS
1. "cast" — ἀποβάλλω (*apoballo*): to throw away; to discard; or to get rid of something no longer desired, needed, or wanted
2. "confidence" — παρρησία (*parresia*): a bold, frank, forthright speech; confidence; audacious; emboldened; openness; extraordinarily frank; a daring to speak what one believes or thinks, possibly even in the face of retribution; boldness; assurance; unashamed confidence; it is a frankness of speech that accompanies unflinching authority

God's Hall of Faith

3. "perdition" — ἀπώλεια (*apoleia*): something ruined, rotten, and decomposing; used to describe the stench of a decaying animal or a dead human body; a loathsome, putrid, vulgar, disgusting, nauseating scent; something in the process of perishing; doomed, rotten, ruinous, or decaying
4. "substance" — ὑπόστασις (*hupostasis*): a compound of ὑπό (*hupo*) and ἵστημι (*histimi*); the word ὑπό (*hupo*) means by or under, and the word ἵστημι (*histimi*) means to stand; literally, to stand by something; the attitude and actions of one who has determined to stand by something promised and refuses to budge from it; a fixed decision that one will be unmoving and he will stay or stand by a person, principle, promise, or territory
5. "hoped for" — ἐλπίζω (*elpidzo*): to actively hope for the fulfillment of something expected; the form used in this verse is continuous, being hoped for, stressing that the manifestation has not come yet
6. "evidence" — ἔλεγχος (*elegchos*): to expose, convict, or cross-examine for the purpose of conviction, as when convicting a lawbreaker in a court of law; the image of a lawyer who brings forth evidence that is indisputable and undeniable, so that the accused person's actions are irrefutably brought to light and as a result the offender is exposed and convicted; also used positively to convince someone of something; used to denote a lawyer who worked diligently to convince people of a new way of thinking or a new way of seeing things; in this case, they weren't trying to convict someone, they were working to convince someone
7. "worlds" — αἰῶνας (*aionas*): from αἰών (*aion*), an age or era; a specific time, age, or era within the past history of mankind; different periods of time
8. "framed" — καταρτίζω (*katartidzo*): to change, to mend, to adjust, or to alter the form or shape of an already existing thing; re-creating, reshaping, remolding, and altering of something that is already in existence; not so much the act of creation, but the act of transformation
9. "the word of God" — ῥήματι Θεοῦ (*rhemati Theou*): by a word from God
10. "translated" — μετατίθημι (*metatithimi*): to translate; to transfer; to remove
11. "not" — οὐχ (*ouch*): emphatically not

12. "found" — εὑρίσκω (*heurisko*): to find or to discover; a discovery made as a result of careful observance; a moment when one makes a surprising or conclusive discovery; points to a discovery made due to an intense investigation, scientific study, or scholarly research
13. "before" — πρό (*pro*): before; earlier
14. "testimony" — μαρτυρέω (*martureo*): a testimony in a court of law; one who is commended by the testimony they gave

SYNOPSIS

When ambassadors and dignitaries from around the world arrived by ship in Saint Petersburg, Russia, during the Romanov reign, they proceeded directly to the renowned Winter Palace to meet with the tsar and his family. The sheer size of this fortress was simply breathtaking. As guests made their way inside, they entered the Jordan Gallery and were escorted up the Jordan Staircase, which was lavishly embellished with more than 11 pounds of gold decorations, exquisite columns, and magnificent paintings that adorned the ceiling.

Once visitors reached the top of the staircase, they were then guided into the Field Marshall Room, which was a massive chamber filled with enormous paintings of famous Russian military heroes. In the center of this commemorative room hung a mammoth chandelier that was forged of bronze and weighed three tons. Still today, it can be seen suspended from the ceiling, and those who guide guests through the palace will usually avoid standing directly underneath it for fear of it falling on them.

Indeed, the Field Marshall Room of the Winter Palace is a most impressive place, honoring the lives of great men who valiantly served to defend and protect the Russian people. In a similar way, God honors the Old Testament heroes of the faith in Hebrews 11 — a chapter known as "God's Hall of Faith." It celebrates the men and women who received a word from God and then chose to align their lives with what He said. They were ordinary people who did extraordinary things — all because they relentlessly stood by God's word in faith and would not let it go.

The emphasis of this lesson:

Enoch was the seventh generation from Adam and the first of the Old Testament heroes listed in God's Hall of Faith. The Bible says he

walked in such close fellowship with God that one day God raptured him into Heaven. His life is mentioned in four books of the Bible.

Why Is It Vital for You To Hold On to Your Faith and Cast Not Away Your Confidence?

Life can be very challenging at times, and when the answer to our prayers is delayed, we can become weary in waiting for God to intervene. Apparently, this is the place the Hebrew believers had come to. After waiting and waiting for a divine breakthrough in their situation, they were tempted to throw in the towel and walk away from their faith. That is why the writer of Hebrews wrote to them and said, "Cast not away therefore your confidence, which hath great recompence of reward" (Hebrews 10:35).

We saw in Lesson 1 that the word "cast" is the Greek word *apoballo*, which means *to throw away, to discard, or to get rid of something no longer desired, needed, or wanted*. It is the same word used to describe the actions of blind Bartimaeus in Mark 10:50 when he was trying to get to Jesus. The Bible says, "And he [Bartimaeus], casting away his garment, rose, and came to Jesus." The words "casting away" are a translation of the Greek word *apoballo*. When Bartimaeus knew Jesus was calling him, he threw off and discarded the covering that was hindering him and made his way to Jesus to receive healing.

In a negative sense, the Hebrew believers were exhausted and extremely discouraged because their prayers had not been answered, and they were ready *to throw away* and *get rid of* their "confidence." This word "confidence" is the Greek word *parresia*, and it describes *a bold, frank, forthright speech; daring to speak what one believes or thinks, possibly even in the face of retribution*. The writer of Hebrews said, "Don't throw away your bold, unashamed confidence and frank confession of faith because it carries a great recompense of reward! Your payday is coming…if you will just hold on."

The writer of Hebrews went on to say, "But we are not of them who draw back unto perdition; but of them that believe to the saving of the soul" (Hebrews 10:39). Those who *withdraw, retreat*, or *back away* from faith in God and His promises will end up in "perdition," which is the Greek word *apoleia*, and it describes *something ruined, rotten, and decomposing*. It was used to describe *the stench of a decaying animal or a dead human body*. When people backslide from faith in God they become sarcastic, cynical, and bitter. Spiritually, they emit an increasingly loathsome, putrid, nauseating scent no one can stand to be around.

Friend, don't let that become your story. Choose to live by faith! In Greek, the word "faith" is *pistis*, and it describes *a persuasion that comes from God that imparts an impulse or "divine spark" to believe*. It is *a force that propels you forward toward a goal*. When you are in faith, you are moving forward and never in retreat. You are gaining new ground, not losing it.

Faith Is the Substance of Things Hoped For, the Evidence of Things Not Seen

In Hebrews 11:1, the Bible says, "Now faith is the substance of things hoped for, the evidence of things not seen." We learned in our second lesson that the word "substance" is the Greek word *hupostasis*, which is a compound of the words *hupo* and *histimi*. The word *hupo* means *by*, and the word *histimi* means *to stand*. When we compound these two words to form *hupostasis*, it literally means *to stand by something*. It is *the attitude and actions of one who has determined to stand by something promised and who refuses to budge from it*. It is *a fixed decision that one will be unmoving and he will stay or stand by a person, principle, promise, or territory*.

Essentially, the Greek word *hupostasis* — translated here as "substance" — describes how faith behaves. To a great degree, it is like a bulldog that has found the bone of its wildest dreams. Energized by voracious desire, that dog resolutely wraps its jaws around that bone as if its life depended on it. No matter how hard you tug or try to pull the bone away, that dog has decided it's going to stand by its bone and never let it go. In the same way, when you're in faith, you doggedly stand by what God said He would do in His Word for your marriage, your family, your business, your church, and your community. Like a bulldog clutching its bone, you continue to tenaciously hold on to God's promises and never let them go.

Again, the Bible says, "Now faith is the substance of things hoped for…" (Hebrews 11:1). The words "hoped for" is a translation of the Greek word *elpidzo*, which means *to actively hope for the fulfillment of something expected*. The form used in this verse is *continuous*, indicating something is being hoped for, stressing that the manifestation has not come yet.

Faith is also "…the evidence of things not seen" (Hebrews 11:1). We saw that the word "evidence" is the Greek word *elegchos*, which is a legal term that was used in a court of law. In this verse, it is used positively and means *to convince someone of something*. It depicts *a lawyer who worked diligently to convince someone*. You might say this "evidence" causes a person to be convinced to the point of conviction. He or she is so convinced by the Word of God and by the Holy Spirit that the promise they have heard is for them, they now speak from a place of strong conviction.

Through Faith 'the Worlds Were Framed'

Continuing his discussion on faith, the writer of Hebrews went on to say, "For by it [faith] the elders obtained a good report" (Hebrews 11:2). The word "elders" is the Greek word *presbuteroi*, and it refers to *the respected ones*. In this case, it indicates *the heroes of faith in the Old Testament*. These individuals obtained a good report, which means these men and women received a word from God.

Hebrews 11:3 adds to this, stating, "Through faith we understand that the worlds were framed by the word of God, so that things which are seen were not made of things which do appear." Again, the word "faith" here is the Greek word *pistis*, and it describes *the unbendable, unbreakable, never-give-up kind of faith that hangs on to and trusts God's promises* — like a bulldog clutches his bone.

It was through that kind of faith, the writer says, "...we understand that the worlds were framed by the word of God..." (Hebrews 11:3). The phrase "we understand" is a translation of the Greek word *nooumen*, which is the plural form of the word *noeo*, meaning *to think* or *to understand*. This word describes *intelligent activity* and could be translated as *we think, we conclude, we rationalize*, or *we understand*.

What do we understand? "That the worlds were framed by the word of God..." (Hebrews 11:3). In this verse, the word "worlds" is a poor translation. It has nothing to do with the creation of the world, which is talked about in the book of Genesis. The word "worlds" is the Greek word *aionas*, which is from the word *aion*, and it describes *an age* or *era*. It is *a specific time, age*, or *era within the past history of mankind*. If this verse were talking about the creation of the world, the writer would have used the word *ges*, which is the word for *planet earth*, or the word *cosmos*, which is the word for *the universe*. The word *aionas* would never be used to describe creation.

How about the word "framed"? Although it too may sound like it refers to creation, it doesn't. It is the Greek word *katartidzo*, and it means *to change*, *to mend, to adjust, or to alter the form or shape of an already existing thing.* Thus, it indicates *re-creating, reshaping, remolding, and altering of something that is already in existence.* It is not the act of creation, but the act of transformation. Then there is the phrase "the word of God." We saw that in Greek, these words literally say, *by a word from God.*

Taking the original Greek meaning of these key words, Hebrews 11:3 would better be translated:

"Through faith — through the unbendable, unbreakable, never-give-up kind of faith that stands by what it's hoping for in God's Word — we understand that the different time periods within the past history of mankind (different generations, decades, centuries, and millennia) have been framed — altered, modified, and radically changed — by individuals who received a word from God, so that things which are seen were not made of things which do appear."

Enoch: The First Inductee To God's Hall of Faith

It's important to note that the entire chapter of Hebrews 11 is talking about people in "God's Hall of Faith." It mentions individuals like Enoch, Noah, Abraham, Sarah, Gideon, and many others just like you who heard a word from God, and then stood by that promise in their generation and time period and changed the course of history.

Take Enoch for example. He was one of the very first prophets of the Old Testament era. He was so accurate in his ability to hear from God and see into the future, that Jude wrote, "And Enoch also, the seventh from Adam, prophesied of these, saying, Behold, the Lord cometh with ten thousands of his saints" (Jude 14). Amazingly, from the early days of human history, Enoch prophetically saw the second coming of Christ!

Actually, the Bible first mentions Enoch in Genesis 5: "And Enoch lived sixty and five years, and begat Methuselah: And Enoch walked with God after he begat Methuselah three hundred years, and begat sons and daughters: And all the days of Enoch were three hundred sixty and five years: And Enoch walked with God: and he was not; for God took him"(Genesis 5:21-24).

Isn't that amazing! Enoch lived in such a close relationship with God that one day God just took him straight to Heaven without experiencing death. Enoch's life was so radical that the writer of Hebrews recorded these same facts from Genesis in the eleventh chapter of his book. He said, "By faith Enoch was translated that he should not see death; and was not found, because God had translated him: for before his translation he had this testimony, that he pleased God" (Hebrews 11:5).

Notice the word "translated" in this verse. It is the Greek word *metatithimi*, and it means *to translate; to transfer; to remove*. In essence, this word "translated" is talking about a *catching away* or *rapture*. Enoch's translation is actually the first rapture recorded in Scripture.

The Bible says he was "not found." The word "not" is the Greek word *ouch*, which means *emphatically not*. And the word "found" is the Greek word *heurisko*, which means *to find* or *to discover*. It is *a discovery made as a result of careful observance; a moment when one makes a surprising or conclusive discovery*. The word *heurisko* — translated here as "found" — points to *a discovery made due to an intense investigation, scientific study, or scholarly research*. So when the Bible says Enoch was "not found," it means that when he disappeared, people began to intensely investigate and seriously search for where he was. But after all their research, they emphatically could not find him.

Hebrews 11:5 also says, "…For before his translation he had this testimony, that he pleased God." The word "before" is the Greek word *pro*, which specifically means *before* or *earlier*. Before Enoch was translated or removed, the Bible says, "…he had this testimony…." In Greek, the word "testimony" is the word *martureo*. It refers to *a testimony in a court of law; one who is commended by the testimony they gave*. It is a form of the Greek word *martus*, which describes *a legal witness who gives a personal testimony in a court of law*, and the evidence he provides is not hearsay; it is a firsthand, personal testimony.

The use of this word indicates that Enoch had personally heard from God that he was not going to see death, and he stood by that word in faith. This was a very personal word.

It's likely that some people may have thought that Enoch had lost his mind. Remember the Greek word *martus* — translated in this verse as the word "testimony"? The word *martus* is where we get the word for a *martyr*, which is *one who suffers unjustly for what he believes*. If Enoch announced that he was never going to die, there were likely skeptics in the community who said he was going crazy. So, he may have suffered a little bit for the word that he received.

But Enoch didn't care because he had a word from God, and he aligned himself with that word and received the manifestation of it against the odds. Through his unbendable, unbreakable, never-give-up kind of faith, he aligned himself with a personal promise he had received, and he saw it manifest in his life.

Friend, God's promise to you is not a fantasy. Enoch was promised a rapture, and he received it. What has God promised you? Healing? A better marriage? A better job? An increase in your finances? Whatever He promised is not a fantasy; it's your personal promise. And if you will align yourself with His Word and stand by it — refusing to move in retreat and continuing to move forward in faith — a great recompense of reward is headed in your direction!

In our next lesson, we will examine what the writer of Hebrews has to say about Noah — the man who the apostle Peter referred to as "a preacher of righteousness."

STUDY QUESTIONS

> Study to shew thyself approved unto God, a workman that needeth not to be ashamed, rightly dividing the word of truth.
> — 2 Timothy 2:15

1. What new fascinating facts did you learn about Enoch?
2. If you had the opportunity to spend one hour with Enoch, what kind of questions would you ask him?

PRACTICAL APPLICATION

> But be ye doers of the word, and not hearers only, deceiving your own selves.
> — James 1:22

1. What promise (or promises) has God made to you personally? Take some time to write them down — even if they seem like they're a fantasy to you. Include any scriptures God has made real to you that support the promise (or promises).

2. What can you do to better align yourself with what God has said to you? How can you fan the fire of your faith? Are there any action steps you can take to help see these promises from God become a reality?
3. One of the ways faith behaves is that it never retreats; it is always moving forward. How about you? Are you moving forward in faith, or are you stationary or steadily moving in reverse? What evidence in your life supports your answer?

LESSON 4

TOPIC
Noah: The Man Who Refused To Give Up

SCRIPTURES
1. **Hebrews 11:1-3,6,7** — Now faith is the substance of things hoped for, the evidence of things not seen. For by it the elders obtained a good report. Through faith we understand that the worlds were framed by the word of God, so that things which are seen were not made of things which do appear. ...But without faith it is impossible to please him: for he that cometh to God must believe that he is, and that he is a rewarder of them that diligently seek him. By faith Noah, being warned of God of things not seen as yet, moved with fear, prepared an ark to the saving of his house; by the which he condemned the world, and became heir of the righteousness which is by faith.
2. **Genesis 6:5-8,11-14** — And God saw that the wickedness of man was great in the earth, and that every imagination of the thoughts of his heart was only evil continually. And it repented the Lord that he had made man on the earth, and it grieved him at his heart. And the Lord said, I will destroy man whom I have created from the face of the earth; both man, and beast, and the creeping thing, and the fowls of the air; for it repenteth me that I have made them. ...But Noah found grace in the eyes of the Lord. ...The earth also was corrupt before God, and the earth was filled with violence. And God looked upon the earth, and, behold, it was corrupt; for all flesh had corrupted

his way upon the earth. And God said unto Noah, The end of all flesh is come before me; for the earth is filled with violence through them; and, behold, I will destroy them with the earth. Make thee an ark of gopher wood...

GREEK WORDS

1. "substance" — ὑπόστασις (*hupostasis*): a compound of ὑπό (*hupo*) and ἵστημι (*histimi*); the word ὑπό (*hupo*) means by or under, and the word ἵστημι (*histimi*) means to stand; literally, to stand by something; the attitude and actions of one who has determined to stand by something promised and refuses to budge from it; a fixed decision that one will be unmoving and he will stay or stand by a person, principle, promise, or territory
2. "elders" — πρεσβύτεροι (*presbuteroi*): elders; the respected ones; in this case, heroes of faith
3. "worlds" — αἰῶνας (*aionas*): from αἰών (*aion*), an age or era; a specific time, age, or era within the past history of mankind; different periods of time
4. "framed" — καταρτίζω (*katartidzo*): to change, to mend, to adjust, or to alter the form or shape of an already existing thing; re-creating, reshaping, remolding, and altering of something that is already in existence; not so much the act of creation, but the act of transformation
5. "the word of God" — ῥήματι Θεοῦ (*rhemati Theou*): by a word from God
6. "without" — χωρίς (*choris*): without, as being outside of a specific place
7. "rewarder" — μισθαποδότης (*misthapodotes*): money, salary, or a payment that is due; can describe a recompense, reimbursement, settlement, or reparation; being reimbursed for an expense a person has paid out of his own pocket in order to get his job done; a full and complete recompense; in this case, the one who pays, rewards, or gives what one has coming to him; a paymaster
8. "being warned" — χρηματίζω (*chrematidzo*): a business transaction; to transact business; to advise or consult with one about important affairs; in this case, to be advised and consulted by God: literally, being divinely advised and warned
9. "not seen as yet" — μηδέπω (*medepo*): not yet, never before

10. "moved with fear" — εὐλαβέομαι (*eulabeomai*): to do something cautiously; to take action urgently and seriously
11. "prepared" — κατασκευάζω (*kataskeuadzo*): he put forth effort to build a vessel, an ark
12. "ark" — κιβωτός (*kibotos*): not a ship, but a wooden box; not for sailing, but for warehousing and saving
13. "to the saving of his house" — εἰς σωτηρίαν τοῦ οἴκου αὐτοῦ (*eis soterian tou oikou autou*): for the explicit purpose of saving his own household

SYNOPSIS

The Romanovs were officially using the marvelous Winter Palace in 1917, the year the Bolshevik Revolution took place. During the long Siberian winters, they had lived and governed from the illustrious Winter Palace. For many years kings and queens and ambassadors from all over Europe journeyed to see the tsar and his family in this enormous fortress, which altogether was about the size of 12 football fields.

After the dignitaries passed through the opulent Jordan Gallery and ascended the stunning Jordan Staircase, they made their way through the Field Marshall Room. This magnificent chamber was adorned with beautiful chandeliers and massive paintings of mighty Russian military leaders who performed gallantly in battle.

From the Field Marshall Room, guests then entered the Memorial Throne Room of Peter the Great, which was first constructed in 1833. Although Peter had died and never actually used the room, it was created to memorialize his life and the important years he reigned in Russia. The walls of this room were covered with crimson velvet, and in the midst of the crimson velvet were medallions of the Regalia and emblems of the Russian Empire, which were spun of pure silver. There was also a resplendent throne that was recessed and arrayed by two Corinthian columns, which were carved of jasper that had been mined in the Euro Mountains. The floor of that room was decked in 16 different kinds of wood including ebony, mahogany, sandalwood, and palm wood.

The purpose of the Memorial Throne Room of Peter the Great and all its lavish decor was to impress visitors and create a feeling that a person of great power and importance was waiting to see them. In a similar way, God created a place of commemoration in the Holy Scriptures. We refer to it as "God's Hall of Faith," and it is found in Hebrews 11. It's filled with snapshots of ordinary people who did extraordinary things, all because they received a word from God and were willing to believe and obey what He said.

The emphasis of this lesson:

Faith is a place. Your place of faith is standing by the promise God made to you and staying in the assignment He gave you. Noah's place of faith was believing in and obeying God's assignment to build the ark to save him, his family, and a sampling of all the animals.

A Review of Hebrews 11:1-3

In **Hebrews 11:1**, the writer opens the chapter talking about what faith is and how it behaves. He wrote:

> **Now faith is the substance of things hoped for, the evidence of things not seen.**

We saw that the word "substance" in Greek is the word *hupostasis*. It is a compound of two Greek words: the word *hupo*, which means *by*, and the word *stasis*, which is a form of the Greek word *histimi*, meaning *to stand*. When these words are compounded, the new word *hupostasis* literally means *to stand by something*. It is *the attitude and actions of a person who has determined to stand by something promised and refuses to budge from it*. This individual has drawn a line in the sand and said, "This has been promised to me, and I will never let go of it. I'm going to stand by this until I receive the manifestation of what has been promised."

You might say the meaning of the word "substance" is a lot like a bulldog that has found the bone of its dreams and has locked its jaws around it and has refused to let it go. It doesn't matter how hard anyone pulls on the bone or tries to retrieve it; that dog is not going to let it loose. In the same way, when you're in faith, you relentlessly stand by what God has said in His Word, and like a bulldog clutching its bone, you continue to tenaciously hold on to His promises until they become a reality in your life.

In **Hebrews 11:2**, the writer continues his discussion on faith saying:

> **For by it [faith] the elders obtained a good report.**

We learned that the word "elders" is the Greek word *presbuteroi*, and it refers to *the respected ones*. In this case, it signifies *the heroes of faith of the Old Testament* who received a word from God and they stood by it (*hupostasis*) until they received the manifestation of it. As a result of their unbendable, unbreakable, never-give-up kind of faith — which refuses to surrender to discouraging and debilitating circumstances — they ended up obtaining a good report (the manifestation of God's promise). That's what will happen to you if you will stand by what God has promised you.

In **Hebrews 11:3**, the writer went on to say:

Through faith we understand that the worlds were framed by the word of God, so that things which are seen were not made of things which do appear.

If we stay true to the context of this chapter, we know this verse is *not* about creation. We saw in verse 2 that the writer talked about the Old Testament heroes and how they obtained a good report through their faith. We must keep that in mind when we come to verse three.

Again, we see that through *faith* — through the unbendable, unbreakable, never-give-up kind of faith — we understand the worlds were framed by the word of God. What is interesting is that the word "worlds" is not the Greek word *ges*, which describes *planet earth*, or the word *cosmos*, which describes *the universe*. It is the Greek word *aionas*, from *aion*, which describes *a specific time, age, or era within the past history of mankind*. And the word "framed" is the Greek word *katartidzo*, which means *to change, to mend, to adjust, or to alter the form or shape of something that already exists*. Hence, it is not so much the act of creation, but the act of transformation.

In light of the meanings of these words, a better translation of this verse would be, "Through unbendable, unbreakable, never-give-up kind of faith, we understand different time periods, different generations within the past history of mankind have been changed, reshaped, and transformed by a word from God."

Remember, the entire eleventh chapter of Hebrews talks about ordinary individuals who received a word from God. They got into agreement with that word, and they — *hupostasis* — tenaciously stood by that word, refusing to give up or give in until it manifested. Through their faith, the power of God was released through them to change their generation and the world.

Friend, that is what will happen to you if you'll get into agreement with what God has spoken. His power will be activated by your faith and begin to flow through you. As a result, your family will be changed, your finances will be changed, your church will be changed, and so will the world around you. God just needs you to get into agreement with Him about what He has promised you and not move from it. That is how powerful you are in Christ when you tenaciously stand by — *hupostasis* — the word you've received and refuse to give up or give in until it manifests.

What Does It Mean To Be 'Without Faith'?

Probably one of the most quoted verses in Scripture is Hebrews 11:6, which says, "But without faith it is impossible to please him: for he that cometh to God must believe that he is, and that he is a rewarder of them that diligently seek him." More than likely, you have heard this verse numerous times and even quoted it yourself. The question is, do you really know what it means?

Most people think the words "But without faith" describe an absence of faith, but that is not true. Notice the second word of the verse — the word "without." It is the Greek word *choris*, and it means *without, as being outside of a specific place*. For example, you can be inside your house or outside your house; you can be in the city or out of the city, but you can't be in both at the same time. This word *choris* —translated here as "without" — is describing faith as a location. That is, you can be *in* faith or *outside* of faith.

What does it mean for you to be *in* faith? Your place of faith is the promise that God made to you. It is your assignment — the location where you need to be. Faith is a place, and you can be *in* faith, or you can move out of faith.

To be "without faith" means to be *outside of faith* — to move out of or to leave your assignment. Consequently, to abandon the promise God gave you is to be in a position where it is impossible to please God. The word "impossible" in Greek indicates it is *absolutely impossible* or it renders one powerless and incapable of pleasing God if he or she moves out of his or her assignment. Again, faith is a place.

Take Rick for example. God called him and his family to Russia. That is their *place of faith*, and if they want to bring pleasure to God, they have to stay where He called them and do what He has told them to do. Likewise, you have to stay in alignment with what God has called *you* to do, and as long as you stay in that place of faith, you will please God.

God Is a Great 'Rewarder'

Hebrews 11:6 goes on to say, "…For he that cometh to God must believe that he is, and that he is a rewarder of them that diligently seek him." The word "rewarder" is the Greek word *misthapodotes*, and it describes *money, salary, or a payment that is due*. It can also describe *a recompense, reimbursement, settlement, or reparation*. It depicts *being reimbursed for an expense a person has paid out of his own pocket in order to get his job done; a full and complete recompense*. In this verse, it denotes *the one who pays, rewards, or gives what one has coming to him; a paymaster*.

This lets us know that when you get into agreement with the promise God has given you — which includes being in the place He has assigned you to be — God, the Paymaster, is going to show up in your life and bring you His rewards, which is the total reimbursement for what you have invested. This is what we see happening in the lives of the people who are listed in "God's Hall of Faith" in Hebrews 11 — including Noah.

Noah Was 'Warned of God' of 'Things Not Seen'

In Hebrews 11:7, the Bible says, "By faith Noah, being warned of God of things not seen as yet, moved with fear, prepared an ark to the saving of his house; by the which he condemned the world, and became heir of the righteousness which is by faith."

What kind of "faith" did Noah have? It was the unbendable, unbreakable, never-give-up kind of faith that refused to budge or back off from what God had spoken. The Bible says Noah was "warned by God."

In Greek, the phrase "being warned" is the word *chrematidzo*, which is a very unique word that describes *a business transaction*. It means *to transact business* or *to advise or consult with one about important affairs*. In this case, it means *to be advised and consulted by God*. The use of this word tells us that Noah had a businesslike relationship with God in which God was the boss and Noah did what he was told. Thus, Noah literally was *being divinely advised and warned* by God "of things not seen as yet."

The phrase "not seen as yet" is a translation of the Greek word *medepo*, which means *not yet, never before*. This makes total sense when we realize what God advised and warned Noah about — a worldwide flood. No one had ever seen a flood of this magnitude. In fact, they hadn't even seen rain. Prior to the flood, the vegetation was watered by a mist that came up from the ground (*see* Genesis 2:5,6).

Furthermore, God instructed Noah to build an ark, which was also something he and everyone else had never seen. Likewise, God told Noah to collect two of every kind of animal — a male and a female — and bring them into the ark. He was also to gather food for the animals and for his family. All these unprecedented tasks were assigned to Noah and his family members, and they required a tremendous amount of resources, time, and labor to execute.

Noah Stayed in His Place of Faith

Indeed, Noah needed to stay in his place of faith — his God-given assignment — for a very long time. It seems the ark's construction took at least 100 years, and Noah's time in the ark itself was just over a year. More than likely, there were times when Noah's wife asked, "Noah, are you absolutely sure God has spoken to you and asked you to do this?" Possibly even his sons said, "Uh, Dad… We're giving our lives for all this. Do you know without question that God spoke to you?"

The truth is, there were forces all around Noah, pulling on him and trying to move him out of his place of faith. This was especially true of the people in the region around him. They had never heard of or seen a flood — neither had they ever seen an ark being built or the parade of animals that gathered in Noah's community. These things seemed extremely bizarre to all the bystanders.

Did people laugh at Noah and his sons? Did they ridicule him and his family and make up all kinds of nasty, derogatory jokes? It is almost a certainty. Remember, Scripture identifies Noah as "a preacher of righteousness" (*see* 2 Peter 2:5). He was a prophet who prophesied that a worldwide flood was going to come and destroy the earth and everything in it. No one had ever even heard of such a thing, which made Noah's words sound even crazier.

Yet regardless of the concert of the world's criticism, the questions from his family, and even the personal concerns that weighed on his mind,

Noah rejected it all and chose to stay in his place of faith. His faith pleased God and it secured his place in God's Hall of Faith.

Moved With Fear, Noah Prepared an Ark

What else does Hebrews 11:7 say about Noah? It says, "...Moved with fear, [he] prepared an ark to the saving of his house; by the which he condemned the world, and became heir of the righteousness which is by faith." The phrase "moved with fear" is a translation of the Greek word *eulabeomai*, and it means *to do something cautiously; to take action urgently and seriously*. Noah knew that he had heard from God, and he was quick to obey. He was not afraid for himself; he simply had a sense of awe and responsibility to do as he had been instructed.

Also notice the word "prepared." It is the Greek word *kataskeuadzo*, and it means *he put forth great effort to build a vessel, an ark*. Thus, Noah put forth everything he had into the construction of the ark, building it exactly according to the plan God had given him. The word "ark" in Greek is *kibotos*. It is not the word for a ship, but *a wooden box*. The ark was *an enormous wooden container* — not for sailing, but for warehousing and saving what it contained.

The book of Genesis provides us a snapshot of the condition of the earth and society and the word God spoke to Noah about it. It says:

> "And God saw that the wickedness of man was great in the earth, and that every imagination of the thoughts of his heart was only evil continually. And it repented the Lord that he had made man on the earth, and it grieved him at his heart. And the Lord said, I will destroy man whom I have created from the face of the earth; both man, and beast, and the creeping thing, and the fowls of the air; for it repenteth me that I have made them. But Noah found grace in the eyes of the Lord.
>
> ...The earth also was corrupt before God, and the earth was filled with violence. And God looked upon the earth, and, behold, it was corrupt; for all flesh had corrupted his way upon the earth. And God said unto Noah, The end of all flesh is come before me; for the earth is filled with violence through them;

and, behold, I will destroy them with the earth. Make thee an ark of gopher wood...."

Genesis 6:5-8,11-14

Looking once more at Hebrews 11:7, it says, "By faith Noah, being warned of God of things not seen as yet, moved with fear, prepared an ark to the saving of his house...." In Greek, the phrase "to the saving of his house" literally means *for the explicit purpose of saving his own household.* Out of the entire population of the earth at that time, only eight people survived the Great Flood: Noah, his wife, his three sons and their wives. Noah and his family were the only ones *not affected* by God's judgment on the world. They were the remnant of righteousness. Noah received a word from God and stood by that word, and his faith and obedience saved his entire household.

Friend, if you want to please God, you have to stay in the place of faith where He called you to be and do what He called you to do. Even if it takes a long time to see the manifestation of what God promised, stand by the word He gave you. God is a Paymaster, and He will show up to reward you with a great recompense if you will stay in your place of faith.

In our next lesson, we will focus on what the writer of Hebrews says about Abraham, the Father of Faith.

STUDY QUESTIONS

> Study to shew thyself approved unto God, a workman that needeth not to be ashamed, rightly dividing the word of truth.
> — 2 Timothy 2:15

1. The Bible says, "But without faith it is impossible to please [God]..." (Hebrews 11:6). Prior to hearing this lesson, what was your perception of this verse? How has the original Greek meaning of the word "without" changed your understanding of this passage and what it means to be "without faith"?
2. Carefully read Genesis 6:1-12 and identify the conditions of the world and the people during Noah's day (also consider Matthew 24:37-39). What was God's reaction to the state of society?
3. Jesus said, "...As it was in the days of Noah, so it will be also in the days of the Son of Man" (Luke 17:26 *NKJV*). In what ways would you say the world today is like it was in Noah's day? Take some time

to pause and ask God to share with you any specific instructions you need for the unprecedented times in which you live.

PRACTICAL APPLICATION

> But be ye doers of the word, and not hearers only, deceiving your own selves.
> —James 1:22

1. Your place of faith is staying in the assignment where God has asked you to serve. If you're going to please God, you have to stay "in faith" — the place where God called you to be. Stop and think: *What has God called me to do? Where has He assigned me to serve? Am I "in faith" or "without (outside of) faith"?* Take a few moments to reflect on these questions and answer honestly.
2. What is your assignment for the *present season* you're in? Are you obediently doing it? If not, why? What has caused you to move "without (outside of) faith"?
3. If you've moved outside the place of faith God has called you to be because of criticism, pressure, or some other force, take time now to repent and ask God for grace to get back into place and stay there until you see the full manifestation of what He has promised.

LESSON 5

TOPIC
Abraham: The Father of Faith

SCRIPTURES

1. **Hebrews 11:1-3,6** — Now faith is the substance of things hoped for, the evidence of things not seen. For by it the elders obtained a good report. Through faith we understand that the worlds were framed by the word of God, so that things which are seen were not made of things which do appear. …But without faith it is impossible to please him: for he that cometh to God must believe that he is, and that he is a rewarder of them that diligently seek him.

2. **Hebrews 11:8-10** — By faith Abraham, when he was called to go out into a place which he should after receive for an inheritance, obeyed; and he went out, not knowing whither he went. By faith he sojourned in the land of promise, as in a strange country, dwelling in tabernacles with Isaac and Jacob, the heirs with him of the same promise: For he looked for a city which hath foundations, whose builder and maker is God.
3. **Genesis 12:1-4** — Now the Lord had said unto Abram, Get thee out of thy country, and from thy kindred, and from thy father's house, unto a land that I will shew thee: And I will make of thee a great nation, and I will bless thee, and make thy name great; and thou shalt be a blessing: And I will bless them that bless thee, and curse him that curseth thee: and in thee shall all families of the earth be blessed. So Abram departed, as the Lord had spoken unto him....
4. **Acts 7:2,3** — And he said, Men, brethren, and fathers, hearken; The God of glory appeared unto our father Abraham, when he was in Mesopotamia, before he dwelt in Charran, and said unto him, Get thee out of thy country, and from thy kindred, and come into the land which I shall shew thee.
5. **Galatians 3:8** — And the scripture, foreseeing that God would justify the heathen through faith, preached before the gospel unto Abraham....

GREEK WORDS

1. "substance" — ὑπόστασις (*hupostasis*): a compound of ὑπό (*hupo*) and ἵστημι (*histimi*); the word ὑπό (*hupo*) means by or under, and the word ἵστημι (*histimi*) means to stand; literally, to stand by something; the attitude and actions of one who has determined to stand by something promised and refuses to budge from it; a fixed decision that one will be unmoving and he will stay or stand by a person, principle, promise, or territory
2. "worlds" — αἰῶνας (*aionas*): from αἰών (*aion*), an age or era; a specific time, age, or era within the past history of mankind; different periods of time
3. "framed" — καταρτίζω (*katartidzo*): to change, to mend, to adjust, or to alter the form or shape of an already existing thing; re-creating, reshaping, remolding, and altering of something that is already in existence; not so much the act of creation, but the act of transformation

4. "the word of God" — **ῥήματι Θεοῦ** (*rhemati Theou*): by a word from God
5. "without" — **χωρίς** (*choris*): without, as being outside of a specific place
6. "impossible" — **ἀδύνατος** (*adunatos*): incapable; impossible; powerless; futile
7. "rewarder" — **μισθαποδότης** (*misthapodotes*): money, salary, or a payment that is due; can describe a recompense, reimbursement, settlement, or reparation; being reimbursed for an expense a person has paid out of his own pocket in order to get his job done; a full and complete recompense; in this case, the one who pays, rewards, or gives what one has coming to him; a paymaster
8. "called" — **καλούμενος** (*kaloumenos*): literally, being called; to call, to invite, or to summon; depicts a summoning that requires the hearer to respond
9. "place" — **τόπος** (*topos*): a real geographical location
10. "receive" — **λαμβάνω** (*lambano*): to receive into one's possession; to take into one's own control and ownership; carries the idea of taking hold of something, grasping onto something, and embracing it so tightly that it becomes your very own
11. "obeyed" — **ὑπακούω** (*hupakouo*): a compound of **ὑπό** (*hupo*) and **ἀκούω** (*akouo*); the word **ὑπό** (*hupo*) means under or by, and the word **ἀκούω** (*akouo*) means I hear; compounded, it pictures one in a subservient position who hears and obeys what is being said to him by a superior; being under authority, listening, and carrying out instructions
12. "not knowing" — **μὴ ἐπιστάμενος** (*me epistamenos*): the word **μὴ** (*me*) means not, and **ἐπιστάμενος** (*epistamenos*) depicts one who is on top of his subject; one who possesses professional knowledge; one who is highly skilled and knowledgeable; but in this case, it is one who is unacquainted, unknowledgeable, unskilled, and unprofessional in where he is going and in what he is doing
13. "whither he went" — **ποῦ ἔρχεται** (*pou erchetai*): where he was going; where he was headed
14. "sojourned" — **παροικέω** (*paroikeo*): to live outside the house; figuratively, to live on the street
15. "strange country" — **ἀλλότριος** (*allotrios*): alien; foreign; strange; unfamiliar; unnatural and even a bit weird

16. "dwelling" — **κατοικέω** (*katoikeo*): settling down into a home; describes a permanent resident
17. "tabernacles" — **σκηνή** (*skene*): tents

SYNOPSIS

The Winter Palace in Saint Petersburg, Russia, was the place where the Romanov family lived and ruled during the winter months and where they welcomed countless kings, queens, and ambassadors from foreign countries. Once the arriving dignitaries made their way into the Jordan Gallery, up the Jordan Staircase, through the Field Marshall Room and the Memorial Room of Peter the Great, they were then guided into one of the largest rooms in the entire palace — the Coat of Arms Hall.

Without question, the Coat of Arms Hall was simply magnificent. Its massive size enabled the accommodation of 2,000 people at a time. If the occasion was for low-level guests, attendees would receive as many as 300 courses of food during the meal. If high-level guests were being entertained, as many as 500 courses would be served, making the event last up to 15 hours!

Like all the other rooms in the Winter Palace, the Coat of Arms Hall was lavishly adorned. There were spectacular chandeliers suspended from the ceiling, exquisite Corinthian columns that lined the walls, and copious amounts of gold ornamentation everywhere. At the entrance of the room were two distinctive statues that were carved out of wood but were painted white to give the appearance of luxurious marble. The purpose of all the breathtaking décor was to impress the guests and remind them of the great wealth and power of the Russian Empire and all the heroes who contributed to its existence.

Just as the Winter Palace is a place commemorating great Russian monarchs and military leaders, Hebrews Chapter 11 is the place in Scripture commemorating the great men and women of faith in the Old Testament. Let's take a few moments to review some of the main points we have learned.

The emphasis of this lesson:

Abraham is the third hero of faith listed in Hebrews 11 and the first person to hear the Gospel. He received a word from God that through him, all the nations of the world would be blessed. Despite harsh living

conditions and many unexpected challenges, he obeyed God and carried out His instructions.

A Summary of Hebrews 11:1-3

In **Hebrews 11:1**, the writer opens the chapter talking about what faith is and how it behaves. He wrote:

> **Now faith is the substance of things hoped for, the evidence of things not seen.**

One of the most important and often misunderstood words in this verse is the word "substance." In Greek, it is the word *hupostasis*, and it is a compound of two Greek words: the word *hupo*, which means *by*, and the word *stasis*, which is a form of the Greek word *histimi*, meaning *to stand*. When we compound these words, the new word *hupostasis* literally means *to stand by something*. It is *the attitude and actions of a person who has determined to stand by something promised and refuses to budge from it.*

The word *hupostasis* — translated here as "substance" — is really a description of how faith behaves. When you are in faith, you are relentlessly standing by God's promises — *hupostasis*. This is the equivalent of saying, "This is my promise and my territory, and I refuse to relinquish it. I'm going to stand by it, defend it, and refuse to budge until I see the manifestation of what God has promised me. When a person is moving in faith, it is clearly apparent because they are standing by what has been promised to them.

Then in **Hebrews 11:2**, the writer goes on to say:

> **For by it [faith] the elders obtained a good report.**

We saw that the word "elders" is the Greek word *presbuteroi*, and it refers to *the heroes of faith of the Old Testament*. As a result of their unbendable, unbreakable, never-give-up kind of faith, these individuals tenaciously stood by — *hupostasis* — the word they received from God until they received a "good report," which is the manifestation of what God promised.

Continuing with the topic of faith, in **Hebrews 11:3**, the writer adds:

> **Through faith we understand that the worlds were framed by the word of God, so that things which are seen were not made of things which do appear.**

Although some have mistaken this verse to be talking about creation, it is actually a continuation of the description of the Old Testament heroes and how they obtained a good report through their faith.

We have noted that the word "worlds" is the Greek word *aionas*, and it describes *a specific time, age, or era within the past history of mankind*. And the word "framed" is the Greek word *katartidzo*, which means *to change, to mend, to adjust, or to alter the form or shape of something that already exists*. Thus, it is not so much the act of creation, but the act of transformation.

Taking into account the meanings of these words — and the fact that the entire eleventh chapter of Hebrews is about the heroes in God's Hall of Faith — a better translation of this verse would be, "Through the unbendable, unbreakable, never-give-up kind of faith, we understand that different time periods and different generations in past human history have been changed, altered, and reshaped by a word from God."

To Please God, You Must Live 'In Faith'

In Lesson 4, we looked at Hebrews 11:6, which is a very familiar yet often misunderstood verse. It says, "But without faith it is impossible to please him: for he that cometh to God must believe that he is, and that he is a rewarder of them that diligently seek him."

We learned that the word "without" is the Greek word *choris*, and it means *without, as being outside of a specific place*. Thus, the phrase "without faith" does not describe an absence of faith — it describes faith as a *location*. For instance, you can be *inside* your house or *outside* your house, but you can't be in both places at the same time. This word *choris* — translated here as "without" — depicts a person who has chosen to be *outside* of faith.

So, *faith is a place*, and your place of faith is God's assignment for you — it is being where God told you to be, doing what He told you to do, believing what He said to believe, and not moving from it at all. This is a picture of *hupostasis*, translated as the word "substance" in Hebrews 11:1. If you are "without faith," you have moved *outside of* your divine assignment. You are no longer believing the word God placed in your heart nor are you doing what He called you to do. And when you're "without (outside of) faith," you are in a position where it is impossible to please God. In Greek, the word "impossible" is the word *adunatos,* and it means *incapable, impossible, powerless, or futile.*

Friend, if you want to please God, stay in your place of faith! Hebrews 11:6 goes on to say, "…For he that cometh to God must believe that he is, and that he is a rewarder of them that diligently seek him." The word "rewarder" is the Greek word *misthapodotes,* and it describes *money, salary, or a payment that is due.* It denotes *being reimbursed for an expense a person has paid out of his own pocket in order to get his job done.* Particularly in this verse, it depicts *the one who pays, rewards, or gives what one has coming to him*; **a paymaster.**

When you get into agreement with what God has promised — when you stay in the place He has assigned you to be — God, the Paymaster, will show up in your life and bring you His rewards. If you're standing by His promises to heal, He will show up with His healing. If you're standing by His promises to provide, He will show up with His provision. This is what we see happening in the lives of the people who are listed in "God's Hall of Faith" in Hebrews 11.

The first person included in God's Hall of Faith is *Enoch.* He was the seventh generation from Adam, and as he walked closely in relationship with God, he received a prophetic word that he would not see death. The Bible says that Enoch stood by that word and achieved a good testimony. He refused to move from God's promise, and as a result, he experienced a personal rapture!

In our last lesson, we learned about Noah and how God spoke to him and alerted him about the total destruction that was coming on the earth. God gave him a word to build an ark for "the saving of his house" (*see* Hebrews 11:7), and Noah stood by that word and demonstrated his faith by obeying God's instructions. As a result of his steadfast faith, Noah altered and reshaped his generation and the world.

By Faith, Abraham Obeyed God

The next well-known hero of the faith listed in God's Hall of Faith is Abraham — the Father of Faith. The Bible says, "By faith Abraham, when he was called to go out into a place which he should after receive for an inheritance, obeyed; and he went out, not knowing whither he went" (Hebrews 11:8).

First, notice the word "called." It is the Greek word *kaloumenos*, which literally means, *being called*. It indicates *to call, to invite, or to summon*. It depicts *a summoning that requires the hearer to respond*. This tells us that Abraham was a *called* man, and when he received God's call, he received a supernatural revelation or enlightenment that his life had a specific purpose.

Scripture then adds that Abraham was called "...to go out into a place..." (Hebrews 11:8). The word "place" is the Greek word *topos*, and it describes *a real geographical location*. When Abraham heard God speaking to him, he knew he needed to get into the right "place" — the right *geographic location* — in order to "receive" his inheritance.

The word "receive" in Greek is a translation of the word *lambano*, which means *to receive into one's possession; to take into one's own control and ownership*. It carries the idea of *taking hold of something, grasping onto something, and embracing it so tightly that it becomes your very own*. The Bible says Abraham "...obeyed; and he went out, not knowing whither he went" (Hebrews 11:8).

In Greek, the word "obeyed" is *hupakouo*. It is a compound of the root word *hupo*, which means *to be under*, and the word *akouo*, which means *I hear*. When these two words are compounded, it pictures *one in a subservient position who hears and obeys what is being said to him by a superior*. It carries the idea of *being under authority, listening, and carrying out instructions*.

The use of the word *hupakouo* — translated in this verse as "obeyed" — lets us know that Abraham first *listened* to God and then *submitted* to His authority, carrying out His instructions. The same response is required of you. If you're going to discover God's assignment for your life, you first need to open your ears. Once you hear God's directions, you will need to submit to His authority and carry out what He says.

According to Scripture, What Did God Say to Abraham?

What's interesting about Abraham's call is that there are details of what God spoke to him recorded in both the Old and New Testaments. Immediately following the chapter on the Tower of Babel and the disbursement of the nations, we find the overview of God's assignment to Abraham. The Bible says:

> **Now the Lord had said unto Abram, Get thee out of thy country, and from thy kindred, and from thy father's house, unto a land that I will shew thee.**
>
> Genesis 12:1

This verse outlines four specific things God asked Abraham to do: (1) leave his country; (2) leave his family; (3) leave his father's home; and (4) go to the land God would show him. If Abraham would obey — if he would *submit* and come under God's authority, *listening* to and carrying out His instructions — God said He would bless Abraham in the following ways:

> **And I will make of thee a great nation, and I will bless thee, and make thy name great; and thou shalt be a blessing: And I will bless them that bless thee, and curse him that curseth thee: and in thee shall all families of the earth be blessed. So Abram departed, as the Lord had spoken unto him....**
>
> Genesis 12:2-4

When we turn to the book of Acts, we find the Holy Spirit speaking through a man by the name of Stephen, who was a deacon in the Early Church. In his powerful address to the High Priest and the Jewish Council, Stephen verbally retraced Israel's history, starting with the details of Abraham's divine call. The Bible says:

> **And he said, Men, brethren, and fathers, hearken; The God of glory appeared unto our father Abraham, when he was in Mesopotamia, before he dwelt in Charran, and said unto him, Get thee out of thy country, and from thy kindred, and come into the land which I shall shew thee.**
>
> Acts 7:2,3

Isn't that interesting? The glory of God appeared to Abraham *before* he lived in Harran. He was a pagan living in the land of Ur of the Chaldeans (*see* Genesis 11:31), worshiping the moon, and then one day God suddenly "appeared" to him. The word "appeared" here is the Greek word *phaneros*, and it describes *something that suddenly manifests*. On that day, God somehow, someway appeared to Abraham in a misty cloud of His glory.

As Abraham was enshrouded in that glorious cloud, God not only gave him the assignment for his life, He also announced to Abraham the message of the Gospel. Galatians 3:8 says, "And the scripture, foreseeing that God would justify the heathen through faith, preached before the gospel unto Abraham, saying, In thee shall all nations be blessed." This means Abraham was the first man in all of history to hear the Gospel.

Abraham's Place of Faith Was Outside of His Comfort Zone

Looking once more at Hebrews 11:8, it says, "By faith Abraham, when he was called to go out into a place which he should after receive for an inheritance, obeyed; and he went out, not knowing whither he went." It is important to point out that Abraham obeyed and went out, "not knowing whither he went."

In Greek, the phrase "not knowing" is *me epistamenos*. The word *me* means *not*, and the word *epistamenos* depicts *one who is on top of his subject*; *one who possesses professional knowledge*; or *one who is highly skilled and knowledgeable*. In this case, it is *one who is unacquainted, unknowledgeable, unskilled, and unprofessional in where he is going and in what he is doing*. Thus, the Bible says that Abraham was *unacquainted, unknowledgeable, unskilled, and unprofessional in* "whither he went," which specifically means *where he was going* or *where he was headed*.

Hebrews 11:9 goes on to say, "By faith he sojourned in the land of promise, as in a strange country, dwelling in tabernacles with Isaac and Jacob, the heirs with him of the same promise." The word "sojourned" is a translation of the Greek word *paroikeo*, which means *to live outside the house*. Figuratively, it means *to live on the street*. A careful study of Abraham's life reveals that he was on the move all the time.

The Bible says he was in a "strange country," which in the Greek describes a place that is *alien; foreign; strange; unfamiliar; unnatural and even a bit weird*. You might say Abraham was like a nomad or a vagabond "dwelling in tabernacles." The word "dwelling" is the Greek word *katoikeo*, which means *settling down into a home* or *becoming a permanent resident*. And the word "tabernacles" is the Greek word *skene*, which is the exact word for *tents*.

The lifestyle God had called Abraham to live was vastly different than the 75 years he had spent in Ur. Genesis 25:7 tells us that Abraham lived 175 years. That means for the remaining 100 years of his life he was living in tents. It is certainly possible that as he wandered around waiting to inherit the Promised Land he had thoughts about returning to his luxurious life in Mesopotamia. Perhaps his wife Sarah asked him a time or two, "Are you sure you heard from God? Back in Ur, we were living at ease, and now we're drifters with no place to call home. Do you really think God wants us to keep doing this?"

Yet in spite of great famines, harsh desert conditions, and wars with enemies, Abraham knew that he had heard from God and he refused to walk away from the great reward God had promised him. He never gave in to the temptation to draw back from his calling. Instead, the Bible says, "He looked for a city which hath foundations, whose builder and maker is God" (Hebrews 11:10).

Friend, don't give up and move out of your divine assignment. Without faith — being outside of the place God has called you — you can't please God. But if you, like Abraham, will stay where God has called you to stay, do what God has told you to do, believe what He has told you to believe, and refuse to budge from it, *payday will come*! Remember, God is a rewarder — He's the ultimate Paymaster — of those who diligently seek Him.

STUDY QUESTIONS

Study to shew thyself approved unto God, a workman that needeth not to be ashamed, rightly dividing the word of truth.
— 2 Timothy 2:15

1. Like Enoch and Noah, Abraham is listed in God's Hall of Faith as a man who received a word from God and stood by it all his life. He is actually mentioned in 27 books of the Bible. From your previous studies, what do you know and appreciate most about Abraham? What new details about his calling and his interaction with God did you learn from this lesson?

2. You may have heard Abraham called the "Father of Faith," but there is another name he is often referred to. Read James 2:23; Isaiah 41:8; and Second Chronicles 20:7 and identify this title.

3. What quality does the apostle Paul celebrate about Abraham in Romans 4:3 and Galatians 3:6? Take a moment to pray and ask the Holy Spirit to help you cultivate this same trait in you.

PRACTICAL APPLICATION

> But be ye doers of the word, and not hearers only, deceiving your own selves.
> —James 1:22

1. To truly discover God's assignment for your life, you first need to be still in His presence and open your ears. Take time now to "Be still, and know that [He] is God..." (Psalm 46:10). Listen carefully to what His Holy Spirit is speaking and revealing to you about your life. If God has spoken to you in the past about your assignment, ask Him to confirm it and clarify anything you are struggling to understand.
2. Once you hear God's instructions, you will need to submit to His authority and carry out what He says. Is there anything God has told you to do that you have left undone? If so, ask Him to forgive you and give you the grace to obediently carry out His orders.
3. God changed the world through the heroes of faith that have gone on before us. Pause and pray, *"Lord, please give me a glimpse of how you are using my obedience to change my generation and the world around me."*

LESSON 6

TOPIC

Sarah: A Woman Who Counted God Faithful

SCRIPTURES

1. **Hebrews 11:1-3,6** — Now faith is the substance of things hoped for, the evidence of things not seen. For by it the elders obtained a good report. Through faith we understand that the worlds were framed by the word of God, so that things which are seen were not made of things which do appear. ...But without faith it is impossible to please

him: for he that cometh to God must believe that he is, and that he is a rewarder of them that diligently seek him.

2. **Hebrews 11:11,12** — Through faith also Sara herself [barren] received strength to conceive seed, and was delivered of a child when she was past age, because she judged him faithful who had promised. Therefore sprang there even of one [Sarah], and him [Abraham] as good as dead, so many as the stars of the sky in multitude, and as the sand which is by the sea shore innumerable.

3. **Genesis 17:1,16,17,19** — And when Abram was ninety years old and nine, the Lord appeared to Abram, and said unto him, I am the Almighty God; walk before me, and be thou perfect. ...And I will bless her [Sarah], and give thee a son also of her: yea, I will bless her, and she shall be a mother of nations; kings of people shall be of her. Then Abraham fell upon his face, and laughed, and said in his heart, Shall a child be born unto him that is an hundred years old? and shall Sarah, that is ninety years old, bear? ...And God said, Sarah thy wife shall bear thee a son indeed; and thou shalt call his name Isaac....

4. **Genesis 18:9-15** — And they said unto him, Where is Sarah thy wife? And he said, Behold, in the tent. And he said, I will certainly return unto thee according to the time of life; and, lo, Sarah thy wife shall have a son. And Sarah heard it in the tent door, which was behind him. Now Abraham and Sarah were old and well stricken in age; and it ceased to be with Sarah after the manner of women. Therefore Sarah laughed within herself.... And the Lord said unto Abraham, Wherefore did Sarah laugh, saying, Shall I of a surety bear a child, which am old? Is any thing too hard for the Lord? At the time appointed I will return unto thee, according to the time of life, and Sarah shall have a son. Then Sarah denied, saying, I laughed not; for she was afraid. And he said, Nay; but thou didst laugh.

5. **Genesis 21:1-3,5,6** — And the Lord visited Sarah as he had said, and the Lord did unto Sarah as he had spoken. For Sarah conceived, and bare Abraham a son in his old age, at the set time of which God had spoken to him. And Abraham called the name of his son that was born unto him, whom Sarah bare to him, Isaac. ...And Abraham was an hundred years old, when his son Isaac was born unto him. And Sarah said, God hath made me to laugh, so that all that hear will laugh with me.

GREEK WORDS

1. "substance" — ὑπόστασις (*hupostasis*): a compound of ὑπό (*hupo*) and ἵστημι (*histimi*); the word ὑπό (*hupo*) means by or under, and the word ἵστημι (*histimi*) means to stand; literally, to stand by something; the attitude and actions of one who has determined to stand by something promised and refuses to budge from it; a fixed decision that one will be unmoving and he will stay or stand by a person, principle, promise, or territory

2. "worlds" — αἰῶνας (*aionas*): from αἰών (*aion*), an age or era; a specific time, age, or era within the past history of mankind; different periods of time

3. "framed" — καταρτίζω (*katartidzo*): to change, to mend, to adjust, or to alter the form or shape of an already existing thing; re-creating, reshaping, remolding, and altering of something that is already in existence; not so much the act of creation, but the act of transformation

4. "the word of God" — ῥήματι Θεοῦ (*rhemati Theou*): by a direct word from God

5. "without" — χωρίς (*choris*): without, as being outside of a specific place

6. "rewarder" — μισθαποδότης (*misthapodotes*): money, salary, or a payment that is due; can describe a recompense, reimbursement, settlement, or reparation; being reimbursed for an expense a person has paid out of his own pocket in order to get his job done; a full and complete recompense; in this case, the one who pays, rewards, or gives what one has coming to him; a paymaster

7. "diligently seek" — ἐκζητέω (*ekzeteo*): to zealously seek; one who seeks something so passionately that he exhausts all his power in his search for it; earnest effort; the idea of being hard-working, attentive, busy, constant, and persistent in one's devotion to what he or she is seeking

8. "barren" — στεῖρος (*steiros*): sterile; unable to produce children

9. "received" — λαμβάνω (*lambano*): to receive into one's possession; to take into one's own control and ownership; carries the idea of taking hold of something, grasping onto something, and embracing it so tightly that it becomes your very own

10. "strength" — **δύναμις** (*dunamis*): power; it carries the idea of explosive, superhuman power that comes with enormous energy and produces phenomenal, extraordinary, and unparalleled results
11. "past age" — **παρὰ καιρὸν ἡλικίας** (*para kairon helikias*): beyond the years of opportunity
12. "judged" — **ἡγέομαι** (*hegeomai*): to deem or to consider
13. "faithful" — **πιστὸν** (*piston*): absolutely faithful; absolutely trustworthy
14. "who had promised" — **τὸν ἐπαγγειλάμενον** (*ton epangeiloamenon*): the one declaring and promising; depicts the declarer and promiser
15. "dead" — **νεκρόω** (*nekroo*): as dead as a corpse; to regard as inoperative; good as dead

SYNOPSIS

It is mind boggling to think that the Russian Empire was once the largest empire in the world, overseeing one-sixth of the earth's surface. The Romanov family ruled the Russian territory for centuries, and in the winter months during the years 1762-1917, they lived in the luxurious Winter Palace in the heart of Saint Petersburg.

As we have noted, this palace was massive in size and breathtaking in its beauty. Ambassadors and dignitaries from Europe and around the world were simply dazzled by its extravagance from the moment they disembarked from their ship and throughout their stay. From the Jordan Gallery and Staircase to the Field Marshall Room and the Memorial Room of Peter the Great, the lavish décor seem to have no end.

The Coat of Arms Room, which could accommodate an extended dining experience for 2,000 guests at a time, was yet another room of great opulence. Surrounding the room were fluted Corinthian columns embellished with more than 18 pounds of gold. Complementing their brilliance were beautiful chandeliers that cascaded from the ceiling. Like all the other rooms in the Winter Palace, the Coat of Arms Room was a place commemorating the rich Russian history.

In Scripture, Hebrews 11 is God's place of commemoration. It is what we call "God's Hall of Faith," honoring the heroes of faith who lived during Old Testament times. They were simple people who received a word from God and then brought their lives into alignment with what He said.

These heroes include people like *Enoch*, who personally received a word from God that he would not see death, and he stood by that word in faith until it manifested. *Noah* is another hero of the faith. He was instructed by God to build an ark to escape the coming worldwide flood. He stood by that word, saving his entire household through his obedience. Also appearing in "God's Hall of Faith" is *Abraham*. He was told to leave his country, his family, and his father's house and go to the land God would show him. Abraham stood by the word God spoke, and his life of obedience is still positively impacting our lives today.

The emphasis of this lesson:
Sarah is the first woman to be included in God's Hall of Faith. Although she was sterile and unable to produce children, she received a word from God that she would give birth to a son, and she stood by that word until in manifested in the birth of Isaac.

A Brief Review of Our Anchor Passage
Hebrews 11:1-3

To help us truly grasp the foundational principles of faith, let's briefly review what we've learned from our anchor passage. **Hebrews 11:1** says, "Now faith is the substance of things hoped for, the evidence of things not seen."

In this verse, understanding the meaning of the word "substance" is very important. It is the Greek word *hupostasis*, which is a compound of the words *hupo* and *stasis*. The word *hupo* means *by* or *alongside*; and the word *stasis* is a form of the Greek word *histimi*, meaning *to stand*. When these words are compounded to form the word *hupostasis*, it literally means *to stand by something*. It is *the attitude and actions of a person who has determined to stand by something promised and refuses to budge from it.*

The word *hupostasis* — translated here as "substance" — describes how faith *behaves*. In many ways, faith acts like a bulldog that has found the bone of its wildest dreams. With great zeal, that dog tenaciously wraps its jaws around that bone, and regardless of how hard you try to pull the bone away from him, that dog has decided to stand by its bone and never let it go. That is the idea being communicated through the word "substance."

When you are in faith, you are relentlessly standing by God's promises — *hupostasis*. Like a bulldog clutching its bone, you continue to tenaciously hold on to His promises until they become a reality in your life.

In **Hebrews 11:2**, the writer goes on to say, "For by it [faith] the elders obtained a good report." We've seen that the word "elders" refers to *the heroes of faith in the Old Testament*. As a result of their unbendable, unbreakable, never-give-up kind of faith, these "elders" — *hupostasis* — resolutely stood by the word they received from God until that which they were believing for manifested. Their faith produced a "good report."

In **Hebrews 11:3**, the writer builds on verse 2, saying, "Through faith we understand that the worlds were framed by the word of God, so that things which are seen were not made of things which do appear." Although it may sound as if this verse is talking about creation, it is actually providing more information on the "elders," or the Old Testament heroes of faith.

The word "worlds" is the Greek word *aionas*, which describes *a specific time, age, or era within the past history of mankind;* or *different periods of time*. And the word "framed" is the Greek word *katartidzo*, which means *to change, to mend, to adjust, or to alter the form or shape of something that already exists*. Hence, it is an act of transformation, not an act of creation. A good illustration of this word would be a potter who is working with clay that he initially molds into a vase. But once he's finished, he decides he doesn't really like the design. So he smashes it and starts all over again. Rather than grab new clay, the potter uses the same clay, altering, reshaping, and fashioning it into something entirely new. That's what the word "framed" means.

Taking into account the meanings of these words — and the fact that the entire eleventh chapter of Hebrews is about the heroes in "God's Hall of Faith" — a better translation of Hebrews 11:3 would be, "Through the unbendable, unbreakable, never-give-up kind of faith, we understand that different periods of time and different generations in past human history have been altered, remolded, and reshaped by the word of God."

In the Greek, the end of this verse actually says *"by a word from God,"* which renders a very different meaning. It indicates that when these elders each received a promise from God and stood by it — *hupostasis* — refusing to let it go, they brought about the release of God's power that changed their generation and their world.

God Will Reward You For Staying in Your Place of Faith

In the previous two lessons, we also examined Hebrews 11:6, which says, "But without faith it is impossible to please him: for he that cometh to God must believe that he is, and that he is a rewarder of them that diligently seek him."

Even though the phrase "without faith" seems to indicate an absence of faith, that is not what it means. The key to understanding the meaning of this verse is found in the word "without," which is the Greek word *choris*, and it means *without, as being outside of a specific place*. This means faith is a real *place* or *location*.

Your place of faith is God's assignment for you — it's being where God told you to be, doing what He told you to do, believing the promise He gave you to believe and not budging from it. You are "without faith," or *outside* your place of faith, when you are *outside* of your assignment and you have abandoned what God promised you. And when you're outside of your place of faith, it is impossible for you to please God.

The last part of Hebrews 11:6 says, "...[God] is a rewarder of them that diligently seek him." The word "rewarder" in Greek describes *money, salary, or a payment that is due*. It means *being reimbursed for an expense a person has paid out of his own pocket in order to get his job done, a full and complete recompense*. In this case, it describes God as the *Great Paymaster — one who pays, rewards, or gives what one has coming to him*. This means if you'll stay in your assignment and continue to stand on the promise (or promises) God gave you and refuse to let go, the day is coming when God — the Great Paymaster — is going to show up and reward you with a great recompense for your faith.

This brings us to the phrase "diligently seek," which in Greek is the word *ekzeteo*, and it means *to zealously seek*. It depicts *one who seeks something so passionately that he exhausts all his power in his search for it*. This word denotes *earnest effort* and carries the idea of *being hard-working, attentive, busy, constant, and persistent in one's devotion to what he or she is seeking*.

The use of the word *ekzeteo* — translated here as "diligently seek" — indicates that staying in your place of faith requires a great deal of hard work. You have to be very committed to staying in your assignment and standing by the promises God gave you. If you pray and ask God for His strength, He will empower you with His Holy Spirit to stay in your place of faith.

Sarah Received Strength From God To Conceive and Give Birth to Isaac

The next person listed in "God's Hall of Faith" is Sarah, the wife of Abraham. The Bible says, "Through faith also Sara herself received strength to conceive seed, and was delivered of a child when she was past age, because she judged him faithful who had promised" (Hebrews 11:11). What's interesting about this verse is that in the original Greek text, there is a word that does not appear in the King James Version. It is the word "barren."

Hence, the first part of this verse in Greek says, "Through faith also Sara herself [barren] received strength to conceive seed…" (Hebrews 11:11). The word "barren" is the Greek word *steiros*, and it means *sterile; unable to produce children*. So when Sarah was physically sterile and unable to produce children, she "received strength to conceive."

The word "received" is a form of the Greek word *lambano*, which means *to receive into one's possession* or *to take into one's own control and ownership*. It carries the idea of *taking hold of something, grasping onto something, and embracing it so tightly that it becomes your very own*. The use of this word tells us that Sarah had to actively engage her faith to receive this strength.

Who gave Sarah strength? God did. Like the other heroes of faith, Sarah received a word from God that she would give birth to a son, and she stood by that word until the promise manifested in her life. The word "strength" in this verse is the Greek word *dunamis*, which means *power*. It carries the idea of *explosive, superhuman power that comes with enormous energy and produces phenomenal, extraordinary, and unparalleled results*.

By faith, Sarah grasped and took hold of the supernatural power she needed to conceive and produce the extraordinary result of having a child "…when she was past age…" (Hebrews 11:11). In Greek, the phrase "past age" is *para kairon helikias*, which means *beyond the years of opportunity*. In the natural, it was physically impossible for Sarah to conceive and give birth to a baby. But she had a word from God, and she held on to that word like a bulldog clutching its bone.

The Bible goes on to say that Sarah delivered her child "...because she judged him faithful who had promised" (Hebrews 11:11). The word "judged" here is a translation of the Greek word *hegeomai*, which means *to deem or to consider*. And the word "faithful" in Greek is the word *piston*, which means *absolutely faithful; absolutely trustworthy*. Sarah took her eyes off of herself and the limitations of her old, feeble body and she put them on God. She *considered* Him to be *absolutely faithful* and *absolutely trustworthy* to do what He said. In fact, the phrase "who had promised" — which is *ton epangeiloamenon* in Greek — means *the one declaring and promising*; it depicts *the declarer and promiser*. Sarah took her eyes off of herself and put them on God, *the Declarer and the Promiser*.

The same is true for you. In order for you to see the full manifestation of what God has promised, you must take your eyes off of yourself — off of your weaknesses, off of your lack of resources, off of your limited strength — and focus them on God, *the Declarer and the Promiser*. He is *absolutely faithful* and *absolutely trustworthy*. He has been faithful and He will be faithful again!

The Birth of Isaac Was First Promised to Abraham

The first time God spoke His promise of a child to Sarah and Abraham (whose name was originally Abram) was in Genesis 17:1. The Bible says, "And when Abram was ninety years old and nine [99 years old], the Lord appeared to Abram, and said unto him, I am the Almighty God; walk before me, and be thou perfect."

God then changed Abram's name to Abraham (*see* verse 5) and made a covenant with him and all of his descendants. He then told Abraham, "And I will bless her [Sarah], and give thee a son also of her: yea, I will bless her, and she shall be a mother of nations; kings of people shall be of her. Then Abraham fell upon his face, and laughed, and said in his heart, Shall a child be born unto him that is an hundred years old? and shall Sarah, that is ninety years old, bear?" (*See* Genesis 17:16,17.)

This news of fathering a child at the age of 100 seemed absolutely impossible to Abraham. In fact, it was laughable. The Bible says he fell to the ground and laughed and spoke to himself "in his heart." But God, who searches and knows all hearts, heard the doubts that Abraham whispered to himself. That is why in verse 19, "...God said, Sarah thy wife shall bear thee a son indeed; and thou shalt call his name Isaac..." (Genesis 17:19).

The name "Isaac" means *laughter*. It was as if God was saying, "If you think this is funny, think again. You're going to have a son, and I want you to name him Isaac because he's going to bring a whole lot of laughter into your lives. When everything is said and done, I'll be the One who gets the last laugh."

When God Gave Sarah the Promise of a Child, She Laughed

Turning to Genesis 18, we see that God appeared once more — this time to Abraham and Sarah at the same time — and reiterated His promise of the birth of Isaac. The Bible says that the Lord spoke to Abraham and said:

"…Where is Sarah thy wife? And he said, Behold, in the tent. And he said, I will certainly return unto thee according to the time of life; and, lo, Sarah thy wife shall have a son. And Sarah heard it in the tent door, which was behind him. Now Abraham and Sarah were old and well stricken in age; and it ceased to be with Sarah after the manner of women. Therefore Sarah laughed within herself…" (Genesis 18:9-12).

Just like her husband Abraham, Sarah laughed at the thought of her conceiving and giving birth to a child. All she could see was the aged condition of her body.

"And the Lord said unto Abraham, Wherefore did Sarah laugh, saying, Shall I of a surety bear a child, which am old? Is any thing too hard for the Lord? At the time appointed I will return unto thee, according to the time of life, and Sarah shall have a son. Then Sarah denied, saying, I laughed not; for she was afraid. And he said, Nay; but thou didst laugh" (Genesis 18:13-15).

Friend, take a moment to chew on what the Lord said in Genesis 18:14: "Is any thing too hard for the Lord?" By posing the question, the Lord was stating a fact: Nothing is too hard for the Lord! Like Sarah, you may think that what God has promised you is too outlandish and impossible to take place. But if God has said it, you can believe He is well able and fully intends to make it happen.

God Makes Good on His Promises

Time passed, and God made good on His promise. The Bible says, "And the Lord visited Sarah as he had said, and the Lord did unto Sarah as he had spoken. For Sarah conceived, and bare Abraham a son in his old age, at the set time of which God had spoken to him. And Abraham called the name of his son that was born unto him, whom Sarah bare to him, Isaac" (Genesis 21:1-3).

What was impossible with Sarah was possible with God! Through faith, she took hold of and received — *lambano* — the superhuman power — *dunamis* — she needed to conceive and give birth to Isaac. She took her eyes off the limitations of her old, feeble body and put them on God, *the Declarer and the Promiser*. She *considered* Him to be *absolutely faithful* and *absolutely trustworthy* to do what He said.

The Bible goes on to say, "And Abraham was an hundred years old, when his son Isaac was born unto him. And Sarah said, God hath made me to laugh, so that all that hear will laugh with me" (Genesis 21:5,6). To this the writer of Hebrews added, "Therefore sprang there even of one [Sarah], and him [Abraham] as good as dead, so many as the stars of the sky in multitude, and as the sand..." (Hebrews 11:12).

The word "dead" in this verse is the Greek word *nekroo*, which means *as dead as a corpse*; *to regard as inoperative* or *as good as dead*. This lets us know that Sarah and Abraham's physical bodies were inoperative, sterile, and incapable of producing a child. But God said they could! He is the One "...Who gives life to the dead and speaks of the nonexistent things that [He has foretold and promised] as if they [already] existed" (Romans 4:17 AMPC).

Friend, you can be *in* faith or *out* of faith. "But without faith it is impossible to please [God]..." (Hebrews 11:6). If you are *outside* of the assignment God gave you, you are incapable of pleasing Him. But if you are *in faith*, doing what He told you to do and holding tightly to His promise, you are positioned to be blessed and be a blessing!

God told Abraham and Sarah they were going to have a baby, and for them to stay in faith they had to — *hupostasis* — stand by the promise that God gave them. This meant they had to deal with their own skepticism and doubts, and diligently pull themselves into alignment with God's promise. But because they did, God showed up as the Great Paymaster and rewarded them with Isaac — the manifestation of His promise. And that's what will happen to *you* if you will stay in a place of faith.

STUDY QUESTIONS

> Study to shew thyself approved unto God, a workman that needeth not to be ashamed, rightly dividing the word of truth.
> — 2 Timothy 2:15

1. What new insights did you learn about Sarah, the Mother of Faith? How did looking at the passages about her life in the Old and New Testament expand your understanding?
2. The Bible says that Sarah "received strength" from God to walk out her divine assignment. Are you weary and exhausted? Do you need supernatural strength to accomplish what God has called you to do? Carefully reflect on His promise to you in Isaiah 40:28-31 and begin to claim it as your own. (Also consider His words in Psalm 28:7,8; 46:1-3; First Chronicles 29:12; and Philippians 4:13.)

PRACTICAL APPLICATION

> But be ye doers of the word, and not hearers only, deceiving your own selves.
> — James 1:22

In order for you to see the full manifestation of what God has promised, you must take your eyes off of yourself — off of your weaknesses, off of your lack of resources, off of your limited strength — and focus them on God, *the Declarer and the Promiser who is absolutely faithful and trustworthy.*

1. Where are your eyes focused right now? Are they on all the symptoms of the sickness? Are they on your dwindling bank account and the mounting bills? Are they on the ungodly leader that is lying about you behind your back and belittling you in front of others? If your eyes are on anything other than God, stop and pray, and ask Him for strength to fix your eyes on Him and Him alone — moment by moment, day by day. We encourage you to reflect on Hebrews 12:1; Psalm 34:5; and Psalm 121.
2. When Sarah laughed at the thought of having a child, the Lord asked her, "Is any thing too hard for the Lord?" (Genesis 18:14). Be honest:

what promise has God given you that seems impossible to become a reality?
3. To strengthen your faith in the knowledge that God keeps His Word, take time to meditate on Numbers 23:19; First Kings 8:56; and Ezekiel 12:25. What is the Holy Spirit saying to you and showing you in these verses?

LESSON 7

TOPIC
Isaac, Jacob, Joseph: Believing for the Next Generation

SCRIPTURES
1. **Hebrews 11:1-3,6** — Now faith is the substance of things hoped for, the evidence of things not seen. For by it the elders obtained a good report. Through faith we understand that the worlds were framed by the word of God, so that things which are seen were not made of things which do appear. ...But without faith it is impossible to please him: for he that cometh to God must believe that he is, and that he is a rewarder of them that diligently seek him.
2. **Hebrews 11:20-22** — By faith Isaac blessed Jacob and Esau concerning things to come. By faith Jacob, when he was a dying, blessed both the sons of Joseph; and worshipped, leaning upon the top of his staff. By faith Joseph, when he died, made mention of the departing of the children of Israel; and gave commandment concerning his bones.
3. **Genesis 50:24-26** — And Joseph said unto his brethren, I die: and God will surely visit you, and bring you out of this land unto the land which he sware to Abraham, to Isaac, and to Jacob. And Joseph took an oath of the children of Israel, saying, God will surely visit you, and ye shall carry up my bones from hence. So Joseph died, being an hundred and ten years old: and they embalmed him, and he was put in a coffin in Egypt.
4. **Exodus 13:19** — And Moses took the bones of Joseph with him...

GREEK WORDS

1. "substance" — ὑπόστασις (*hupostasis*): a compound of ὑπό (*hupo*) and ἵστημι (*histimi*); the word ὑπό (*hupo*) means by or under, and the word ἵστημι (*histimi*) means to stand; literally, to stand by something; the attitude and actions of one who has determined to stand by something promised and refuses to budge from it; a fixed decision that one will be unmoving and he will stay or stand by a person, principle, promise, or territory

2. "worlds" — αἰῶνας (*aionas*): from αἰών (*aion*), an age or era; a specific time, age, or era within the past history of mankind; different periods of time

3. "framed" — καταρτίζω (*katartidzo*): to change, to mend, to adjust, or to alter the form or shape of an already existing thing; re-creating, reshaping, remolding, and altering of something that is already in existence; not so much the act of creation, but the act of transformation

4. "the word of God" — ῥήματι Θεοῦ (*rhemati Theou*): by a direct word from God

5. "without" — χωρίς (*choris*): without, as being outside of a specific place

6. "rewarder" — μισθαποδότης (*misthapodotes*): money, salary, or a payment that is due; can describe a recompense, reimbursement, settlement, or reparation; being reimbursed for an expense a person has paid out of his own pocket in order to get his job done; a full and complete recompense; in this case, the one who pays, rewards, or gives what one has coming to him; a paymaster

7. "diligently seek" — ἐκζητέω (*ekzeteo*): to zealously seek; one who seeks something so passionately that he exhausts all his power in his search for it; earnest effort; the idea of being hard-working, attentive, busy, constant, and persistent in one's devotion to what he or she is seeking

8. "blessed" — εὐλογέω (*eulogeo*): from εὐ (*eu*) and λόγος (*logos*); the word εὐ (*eu*) means good, swell, well, and depicts something wonderful or pleasurable; the word λόγος (*logos*); means words; compounded, to speak good or pleasurable words; good words that confer a blessing

9. "dying" — ἀποθνήσκω (*apothnesko*): withering away; wasting away; pictures one breathing his last breath

10. "worshipped" — προσκυνέω (*proskuneo*): a compound of the words πρός (*pros*) and κυνέω (*kuneo*); the word πρός (*pros*) means toward, and the word κυνέω (*kuneo*) means to kiss; when compounded, to fall on the ground toward someone and to kiss; used to depict a person's worshipful position before the Lord; pictures one who has prostrated himself, either outwardly or inwardly, bowing in his heart before God and worshiping Him with kisses in intimate adoration
11. "leaning" — ἐπί (*epi*): upon, as in leaning
12. "staff" — ῥάβδος (*rhabdos*): a staff, scepter, a symbol of authority
13. "died" — τελευτάω (*teleutao*): finishing; coming to conclusion; having reached his end
14. "mention" — μνημονεύω (*mnemoneuo*): denoted a written record to memorialize a person's actions; a memorial that was intended to be permanent; to remember, recollect, mention, commemorate, or to memorialize
15. "departing" — ἔξοδος (*exodos*): the exodus
16. "commandment" — ἐντέλλομαι (*entellomai*): to command concerning the end-objective; to instruct how or where something should end

SYNOPSIS

History shows that the Romanov family officially lived in the Winter Palace during the winter months in the years leading up to the Bolshevik Revolution in 1917. Newly arriving dignitaries and ambassadors were awed by the magnificence of this massive fortress. Even those who came from Europe had never seen opulence on this level.

As guests made their way through the Jordan Gallery, up the Jordan Staircase, through the Field Marshall Room, and the Memorial Room of Peter the Great, they entered the Coat of Arms Room, which was dedicated to the remembrance of the ruling families of Russia and all the contributions they had made to protect and advance the Russian Empire. Like the Jordan Staircase, the Coat of Arms Room was decked with more than 18 pounds of gold embellishments.

The next room visitors entered was called the Military Gallery of the War of 1812. It was a chamber commemorating Russia's victorious conflict with Napoleon. The walls of this gallery contain 332 portraits of the generals who fought in the war under Russian Emperor Alexandra I. Interestingly, 13 of the picture frames that hang on the walls are empty because the generals they belonged to were no longer living at the time the portraits were painted.

At the far end of the gallery hangs a portrait of Emperor Alexander I himself who led the charge against Napoleon and drove him out of Russia. In 1837, just ten years after the completion of the Military Gallery, it was destroyed by a massive fire. Years later it was reconstructed to its original state, which can still be visited today.

The intention of this hall was to memorialize the emperor and the generals who fought valiantly with him in the war and accomplished great things. Similarly, the generals of faith in the Old Testament who pioneered the path that we as believers walk on today are memorialized in Hebrews 11. It is what we call "God's Hall of Faith." In these verses, God commemorates simple people who did significant things. They received a word from Him and got into alignment with what He asked them to do, and because they obeyed, they effectively changed their generation and the world.

The emphasis of this lesson:

Isaac, Jacob, and Joseph are also listed in "God's Hall of Faith." They are a clear example of what we are to do with our faith as we get older and have not seen all that God has promised come to pass. Instead of letting go of our faith, we are to shift our faith and begin to believe for God's promises to come to pass in the lives of our children and grandchildren.

A SUMMARY OF THE KEY WORDS IN HEBREWS 11

Faith Is the 'Substance'

In Hebrews 11:1-3, the writer lays a foundation for what he is going to talk about in the entire chapter. He opens in Hebrews 11:1 saying, "Now faith is the substance of things hoped for, the evidence of things not seen."

We have noted that the word "substance" is the Greek word *hupostasis*, which is a compound of the words *hupo* and *stasis*. The word *hupo* means *by*, and the word *stasis* is a form of the Greek word *histimi*, which means *to stand*. When we join these words to form the word *hupostasis*, it literally means *to stand by something*. It is *the attitude and actions of a person who has determined to stand by something promised and refuses to budge from it.*

Furthermore, it is *a fixed decision that one will be unmoving and he will stay or stand by a person, principle, promise, or territory*.

Rather than define what "faith" is, the word *hupostasis* — translated here as "substance" — actually describes how faith *behaves*. Again, faith is like a bulldog that has found the bone of its dreams. It tenaciously wraps its jaws around that bone, and regardless of how hard one tries to pull the bone away, that dog has decided to unflinchingly stand by it and never let it go. That is the idea being communicated through the word "substance."

By Faith, the 'Elders' Obtained a Good Report

In Hebrews 11:2, the writer went on to say, "For by it [faith] the elders obtained a good report." We've noted that the word "elders" refers to *the heroes of faith in the Old Testament*. Through their unbendable, unbreakable, never-give-up kind of faith, these "elders" determinedly stood by — *hupostasis* — the word they received from God until that which they were believing for manifested. Their faith produced a "good report."

Through Faith the 'Worlds Were Framed'

Then in Hebrews 11:3, the writer declared, "Through faith we understand that the worlds were framed by the word of God, so that things which are seen were not made of things which do appear." Although it may sound as if this verse is talking about creation, it is actually providing more information on the "elders," or the Old Testament heroes of faith.

In Greek, the word "worlds" is *aionas*, and it describes *a specific time, age, or era within the past history of mankind*. And the word "framed" is the Greek word *katartidzo*, which means *to change, to mend, to adjust, or to alter the form or shape of something that already exists*. Thus, it is not so much the act of creation, but the act of transformation.

Taking into account the meanings of these words, a better translation of Hebrews 11:3 would be: "Through faith — the unbendable, unbreakable, never-give-up kind of faith that is unwaveringly standing by what has been promised — we understand that different time periods and different generations in past human history have been altered, remolded, and reshaped by individuals who received a word from God."

'Without Faith' It Is Impossible To Please God

Hebrews 11:6 says, "But without faith it is impossible to please him...." We have seen that the word "without" is the Greek word *choris*, and it means *without, as being outside of a specific place*. It describes *faith as a location*. In this verse, it is talking about a person who is *outside* of faith, which means they have walked away from or abandoned the promise, or promises, God spoke to them and are no longer doing what He asked them to do.

For you to be *in* your place of faith means you are holding tightly to the promises God made to you and you are actively carrying out the assignment He gave you. If you are "without faith" — if you've left your assignment and abandoned God's promises to you — it will be impossible to please Him.

God Is a 'Rewarder' of Them That 'Diligently Seek' Him

The verse goes on to say, "…For he that cometh to God must believe that he is, and that he is a rewarder of them that diligently seek him" (Hebrews 11:6). In Greek, the word "rewarder" describes *money, salary, or a payment that is due*. In this particular verse, it depicts God as the *Great Paymaster — one who pays, rewards, or gives what one has coming to him*. This means if you'll stay in your assignment and continue to stand on God's promises and refuse to let go, the day is coming when He is going to show up as the Great Paymaster and reward you with a great recompense for your faith.

This brings us to the phrase "diligently seek," which in Greek is the word *ekzeteo*, and it means *to zealously seek*. It depicts *one who seeks something so passionately that he exhausts all his power in his search for it*. This word denotes *earnest effort* and carries the idea of *being hard-working, attentive, busy, constant, and persistent in one's devotion to what he or she is seeking*. The inclusion of the word *ekzeteo* — translated here as "diligently seek" — indicates that staying in your place of faith requires a great deal of hard work.

Enoch, Noah, Abraham, and Sarah Are All Heroes of the Faith

In our previous lessons, we have looked at four ordinary individuals who did extraordinary things through their unbendable, unbreakable, never-give-up faith. The first person was Enoch. He had received a word from God that he would not see death, and he stood by that word in faith until it manifested. Next, we saw Noah, who the Bible says was "warned of God of things not seen" (Hebrews 11:7). God instructed Him to prepare an ark to escape the coming worldwide flood. Even though society sneered and laughed at him for what he was doing, he refused to budge from his assignment. Instead, he acted on God's word in faith and saved his whole household.

In Lesson 5, we looked at the life of Abraham — the wealthy pagan who was living luxuriously in the land of Mesopotamia. One day he suddenly received a visitation from God, who told him to leave his country, his family, and his father's house and go to the land He would show him. Abraham aligned himself with the word he had received, and even though it took a very long time for God's promise to come to pass, he refused to budge from what God said until it was manifested.

In our last lesson, we looked at Sarah's example. In Hebrews 11:11, the Bible explicitly says that she was physically sterile and unable to produce children. Nevertheless, she had received a word from the Lord that she would have a baby. So she reached out in faith and took a hold of the dynamic power of God, and it enabled her body to conceive and give birth to Isaac.

In the natural, all these deeds were impossible. But these individuals had heard a word from God, and they aligned themselves with what He said, tenaciously standing by it in faith. And while the circumstances of life and the people around them tried to pull them out of their place of faith, they refused to move away.

Friend, I don't know what God has promised you, but you can be sure that the devil — and people around you — will try to force you out of your place of faith. Therefore, you have to decide and resolve: "I'm not budging, and I'm not flinching. I'm going to keep believing that what God told me will come to pass, and I'm not moving until I receive the full manifestation of God's promise to my life."

Isaac and Jacob Shifted Their Faith and Chose To Speak Blessings on the Next Generation

Who else is listed in "God's Hall of Faith"? That would be Isaac, the son of Abraham and Sarah. The Bible says, "By faith Isaac blessed Jacob and Esau concerning things to come" (Hebrews 11:20). The word "blessed" is the Greek word *eulogeo*, which is from the words *eu* and *logos*. The word *eu* means *good, swell, well*, and depicts something *wonderful or pleasurable*; and the word *logos* means *words*. When *eu* and *logos* are compounded to form the word *eulogeo*, it means *to speak good or pleasurable words; good words that confer a blessing*.

When Isaac had come to the end of his life and he knew he was about to die, all the things he was believing God to do had not yet come to pass. Rather than giving into disappointment and despondency, Isaac shifted his faith and began to believe that God's promises would come to pass on the next generation. He released his faith by opening his mouth and speaking "blessings" — *good, pleasurable words* — on his sons Jacob and Esau. Again, Isaac spoke these blessings "by faith" — by the unbendable, unbreakable, never-give-up kind of faith.

Then when we come to Hebrews 11:21, the focus shifts to Jacob. The Bible says, "By faith Jacob, when he was a dying, blessed both the sons of Joseph; and worshipped, leaning upon the top of his staff." The word "dying" here is the Greek word *apothnesko*, which literally means *withering away* or *wasting away*. It pictures *one breathing his last breath*.

Here again is the picture of a man reaching the end of his life and not seeing the full manifestation of what he was believing God to do. Instead of getting upset and complaining that things didn't work out the way he wanted, Jacob followed the example of his father and shifted his faith to the next generation by speaking blessings on the sons of Joseph. Again, the word "blessed" is the Greek word *eulogeo*, which means *to speak good or pleasurable words; good words that confer a blessing*.

Along with blessing his grandchildren, the Bible says that Jacob "…worshipped, leaning upon the top of his staff" (Hebrews 11:21). In Greek, the word "worshipped" is *proskuneo*, which is a compound of the words *pros* and *kuneo*. The word *pros* means *toward*, and the word *kuneo* means *to kiss*. When compounded to form the word *proskuneo*, it means *to fall on the ground toward someone and to kiss*. This word is used to depict *a person's worshipful position before the Lord*. It pictures *one who has prostrated himself, either outwardly or inwardly, bowing in his heart before God and worshiping Him with kisses in intimate adoration*.

By including this word, we see that when Jacob was dying, he chose to use the last bit of his life's energy to intimately worship God. And he did this while "leaning upon the top of his staff" (Hebrews 11:21). The word "leaning" is the Greek word *epi*, which means *upon, as in leaning*. And the word "staff" is the Greek word *rhabdos*, and it describes *a staff, scepter, a symbol of authority*. The fact that Jacob was leaning on his staff shows his frail condition as he neared death. Yet regardless of how frail he was, Jacob chose to worship God and shift his faith to speak blessings on the next generation.

Joseph's Final Words Were Prophetic

In the very next verse, the writer of Hebrews shifts his focus onto Joseph and says, "By faith Joseph, when he died, made mention of the departing of the children of Israel; and gave commandment concerning his bones" (Hebrews 11:22).

In Greek, the word for "died" is *teleutao*, and it means *finishing*. It denotes *coming to a conclusion*; *having reached his end*. When Joseph had *reached the end* of his life, he "…made mention of the departing of the children of Israel…" (Hebrews 11:22). The word "mention" is a translation of the Greek word *mnemoneuo*, and it denoted *a written record to memorialize a person's actions*. It described *a memorial that was intended to be permanent*. The word *mnemoneuo* — translated here as "mention" — can also mean *to remember, recollect, mention, commemorate, or to memorialize*.

This verse lets us know that when Joseph made his statement about "the departing of the children of Israel," he wanted everyone to remember what he said and fix it in their minds. The word "departing" in Greek is the word *exodos*, which refers to *the exodus* of the Israelites. Joseph prophesied that they would depart from Egypt, and he was so sure of it that he gave them a "commandment" concerning his bones.

The word "commandment" is the Greek word *entellomai*, which means *to command concerning the end-objective; to instruct how or where something should end*. Joseph knew his flesh would already be gone and that only his bones would be left, which meant the departure would not occur soon. Nevertheless, he knew it would eventually take place — and it did take place about 200 years after Joseph's death.

This verse captures a declaration of Joseph's faith — that the children of Israel would depart from Egypt. It was Joseph's faith request that when they left, his bones would be carried home, and his request was carried out. The Bible says, "And Moses took the bones of Joseph with him" (Exodus 13:19).

It is amazing that Isaac, Jacob, and Joseph all stood in faith for what God had promised and refused to let go of it. They each stood by the promise that had been made to them, and when they came to the end of their lives and they hadn't seen all of it fulfilled, they didn't just throw their hands up and say, "Well, this didn't work." Instead, they chose to shift their faith toward the next generation. They said, "What has been promised to me is going to happen — even if it doesn't happen in my lifetime. I believe it's going to happen for my kids and my grandkids."

Friend, maybe that's what you need to do. Rather than lament over the promises of God that have not happened in your life, shift your faith to the next generation. Open your mouth and begin to speak a blessing over your family, because they're going to be inheritors of all the promises that God has made to you.

STUDY QUESTIONS

Study to shew thyself approved unto God, a workman that needeth not to be ashamed, rightly dividing the word of truth.
— 2 Timothy 2:15

1. What new facts did you learn about the lives of Isaac, Jacob, and Joseph?
2. How we use our words is very important. The Bible says that Isaac and Jacob released their faith by speaking words of blessing upon the next generation. To get a better understanding of the power of your words, read what the Bible says in these passages:
   - Proverbs 18:20,21
   - Psalm 34:11-13; 1 Peter 3:10,11
   - Proverbs 13:3 and 21:23
   - Ephesians 4:29; Colossians 4:6
3. If you've ever wondered whether or not God uses people in their old age, He does. Read the brief snapshot of the lives of Simeon and Anna in Luke 2:25-38. What can you learn from their lives about how God works in us and through us, even in our senior years?

PRACTICAL APPLICATION

> But be ye doers of the word, and not hearers only,
> deceiving your own selves.
> —James 1:22

1. Have there been things that God has spoken to you that have not come to pass yet? If so, what are they?
2. How might you shift your faith to the next generation and help position them to see God's promises come to pass in *their* day?

LESSON 8

TOPIC

Moses: A Man With an Assignment

SCRIPTURES

1. **Hebrews 11:1,2,6** — Now faith is the substance of things hoped for, the evidence of things not seen. For by it the elders obtained a good report. ...But without faith it is impossible to please him: for he that cometh to God must believe that he is, and that he is a rewarder of them that diligently seek him.

2. **Hebrews 11:23-29** — By faith Moses, when he was born, was hid three months of his parents, because they saw he was a proper child; and they were not afraid of the king's commandment. By faith Moses, when he was come to years, refused to be called the son of Pharaoh's daughter; choosing rather to suffer affliction with the people of God, than to [have and] enjoy the pleasures of sin for a season; esteeming the reproach of Christ greater riches than the treasures in Egypt: for he had respect unto the recompence of the reward. By faith he forsook Egypt, not fearing the wrath of the king: for he endured, as seeing him who is invisible. Through faith he kept the passover, and the sprinkling of blood, lest he that destroyed the firstborn should touch them. By faith they passed through the Red Sea as by dry land: which the Egyptians assaying to do were drowned.

GREEK WORDS

1. "substance" — ὑπόστασις (*hupostasis*): a compound of ὑπό (*hupo*) and ἵστημι (*histimi*); the word ὑπό (*hupo*) means by and the word ἵστημι (*histimi*) means to stand; literally, to stand by something; the attitude and actions of one who has determined to stand by something promised and refuses to budge from it; a fixed decision that one will be unmoving and he will stay or stand by a person, principle, promise, or territory
2. "without" — χωρίς (*choris*): without, as being outside of a specific place
3. "rewarder" — μισθαποδότης (*misthapodotes*): money, salary, or a payment that is due; can describe a recompense, reimbursement, settlement, or reparation; being reimbursed for an expense a person has paid out of his own pocket in order to get his job done; a full and complete recompense; in this case, the one who pays, rewards, or gives what one has coming to him; a paymaster
4. "diligently seek" — ἐκζητέω (*ekzeteo*): to zealously seek; one who seeks something so passionately that he exhausts all his power in his search for it; earnest effort; the idea of being hard-working, attentive, busy, constant, and persistent in one's devotion to what he or she is seeking
5. "proper child" — ἀστεῖος (*asteios*): polished; elegant; sophisticated; unusual
6. "refused" — ἀρνέομαι (*arneomai*): to deny, to disown, to reject, to refuse, or to renounce; referred to a person who disavowed, forsook, walked away from, or washed one's hands of another person or group of people; such denials were often accompanied by ridicule or persecution
7. "choosing" — αἱρέω (*haireo*): choose; prefer; depicts a personal choice or preference that sets one apart from others
8. "suffer affliction with" — συγκακουχέω (*sunkakoucheo*): depicts joint suffering; to suffer bad things in partnership with others
9. "enjoy" — ἀπόλαυσις (*apolausis*): enjoyment; benefits
10. "season" — πρόσκαιρος (*proskairos*): for a limited season; for a temporary season
11. "esteeming" — ἡγέομαι (*hegeomai*): to deem or to consider

12. "reproach" — ονειδισμός (*oneidismos*): insults; language intended to injure, harm, hurt, or damage; words that damage one's reputation
13. "riches" — πλούσιος (*plousios*): wealth so great it cannot be tabulated; abundant or vast wealth; extreme riches; unlimited wealth; incredible abundance; opulence; extravagant lavishness; someone who possesses incredible abundance, extreme wealth, and enormous affluence; magnificent wealth
14. "treasures" — θησαυρός (*thesauros*): a word describing a treasure, a treasury, a treasure chamber, or a place of safekeeping where riches and fortunes are kept; it presents the idea of a special place designed as a repository for massive riches and wealth
15. "respect" — ἀποβλέπω (*apoblepo*): to lift one's eyes to look away to see something else
16. "recompense of the reward" — μισθαποδοσία (*misthapodosia*): the word for money, salary, or a payment that is due; primarily used to denote a payment, salary, or reward given for a job performed; can describe a recompense, reimbursement, settlement, or reparation; being reimbursed for an expense a person has paid out of his own pocket in order to get his job done; a full and complete recompense
17. "forsook" — καταλείπω (*kataleipo*): to abandon and leave behind
18. "wrath" — θυμός (*thumos*): portraying a person who suddenly flares up and loses control; deep-seated anger; an outburst; a person who boils with anger and blows up, erupting in an ugly outburst that negatively affects other people
19. "endured" — καρτερέω (*kartereo*): steadfast; preserve; continue undeterred
20. "passed through" — διαβαίνω (*diabaino*): literally, walk through or step through
21. "as by dry land" — ὡς διὰ ξηρᾶς γῆς (*hos dia zeras ges*): as through dried up earth

SYNOPSIS

In 1812 there was a dreadful battle between Napoleon and the country of Russia. Napoleon had entered into Russia and declared that he was going to seize the capital of Moscow and the city of Saint Petersburg and take all of its treasures. But in that crucial moment, Alexander I, who was the

Emperor of Russia, mustered his military forces and drove Napoleon out of the land.

Although the battle was enormous, Russia won. To commemorate their victory over Napoleon, the Romanov family constructed the Military Gallery of 1812 in the Winter Palace. Within the halls of this beautiful room, Alexander I and the 332 generals who heroically fought with him in the war are memorialized for successfully crushing Napoleon and his forces.

Pictures of each of these generals hang on the walls of this gallery. What's interesting is that 13 of these picture frames are empty because the generals, whose portraits were to be hung in them, were deceased at the time all the other portraits were painted. But because no one wanted to forget them and their contribution to the victory, the empty frames hang on the walls to commemorate these men. We may not know their faces, but what they did has never been forgotten.

It's that way with God too. Although we don't know all the faces of the believers who have fought spiritual battles before us, God has never forgotten them. In fact, when you come to Hebrews 11, which we call "God's Hall of Faith," many of these heroes of the faith are memorialized. They each received a word from God and brought their lives into alignment with Him. As a result of their obedience, they ended up in "God's Hall of Faith." And God has room for you, as well, in His Hall of Faith!

The emphasis of this lesson:

By faith, Moses renounced that he was the son of Pharaoh's daughter, exchanging the benefits of royalty for suffering with God's people. He considered the reproach of Christ greater riches than all of Egypt's treasures and focused his eyes on the great reward God would give him. By faith, he abandoned Egypt and embraced God's call on his life.

Faith Is Standing By Things Hoped For

Hebrews 11:1 is a foundational verse regarding the subject of faith that says, "Now faith is the substance of things hoped for, the evidence of things not seen." We have noted that understanding the word "substance" is vital to understanding the rest of the chapter. The word "substance" is the Greek word *hupostasis*, which is a compound of the word *hupo* and *histimi*. The word *hupo* means *by* and the word *histimi* means *to stand*.

When these words are compounded, it literally means *to stand by something*. It depicts *the attitude and actions of one who has determined to stand by something promised and refuses to budge from it*. It is *a fixed decision that one will be unmoving and he will stay or stand by a person, principle, promise, or territory*.

Thus, when we read Hebrews 11:1, we see how faith *behaves*. It is a bulldog attitude that says, "I'm never going to let go of this promise nor am I going to budge from where God has called me. I'm going to stand by this until I see the manifestation or for the rest of my life if need be." When a person is moving in faith, you can recognize it by their behavior. Faith never stops and never quits. Hence, Hebrews 11:1 could be translated, *"Faith is standing by things hoped for."*

Outside of Your Place of Faith, You Cannot Please God

Another foundational verse regarding faith is Hebrews 11:6, which says, "But without faith it is impossible to please him [God]...." When many people hear the words "But without faith," they think it describes an absence of faith, but that is not what it means. The word "without" is the Greek word *choris*, and it means *without, as being outside of a specific place*. For example, you can be inside your house or outside your house, but you can't be inside and outside your house at the same time.

This word *choris* —translated here as "without" — is describing a person who is *outside* of faith. At one time they were living in a place of faith, but for some reason they chose to move out of faith. Your place of faith is holding onto the promises God gave you and staying active in the assignment where he has called you to serve. If you cast away your confidence, walking away from God's promises and His assignment, you cannot please Him. Therefore, if you want to please God, you have to choose to stay in your place of faith.

If You Diligently Seek God, He Will Reward You

Hebrews 11:6 goes on to say, "...For he that cometh to God must believe that he is, and that he is a rewarder of them that diligently seek him." We have seen that the Greek word for "rewarder" in this verse depicts God as the *Great Paymaster* — *one who pays, rewards, or gives what one has coming to him*. This means if you'll stay in your place of faith — holding tightly to God's promises and being actively committed to the assignment He's given you — the day is coming when He is going to show up as the Great Paymaster and reward you with a great recompense for your faith.

This brings us to the phrase "diligently seek," which in Greek is the word *ekzeteo*, and it means *to zealously seek*. It pictures *one who seeks something so passionately that he exhausts all his power in his search for it*. This word denotes *earnest effort* and carries the idea of *being hard-working, attentive, busy, constant, and persistent in one's devotion to what he or she is seeking*. The use of the word *ekzeteo* in this verse means that staying in your place of faith requires a great deal of hard work.

Moses Was a Mighty Man of Faith

He Was a 'Proper Child'

The next Old Testament character mentioned in "God's Hall of Faith" is *Moses*. Hebrews 11:23 says, "By faith Moses, when he was born, was hid three months of his parents, because they saw he was a proper child; and they were not afraid of the king's commandment." When the Bible says "by faith," it is again referring to the unbendable, unbreakable, never-give-up faith that stands by the promises of God. It was through this type of faith that the parents of Moses hid him for three months "… because they saw he was a proper child…" (Hebrews 11:23).

In Greek, the word "proper child" is *asteios*, and it means *polished; elegant; sophisticated; or unusual*. The moment Moses' parents saw him at his birth, they immediately saw that there was something unique and unusual about him. At that time, Pharaoh had commanded that every Hebrew male child born was to be killed (*see* Exodus 1:15,16). But because Moses' parents were living by faith, they were not afraid of Pharaoh's command.

He 'Refused' To Be Called the Son of Pharaoh's Daughter

The Bible says when they could no longer hide Moses, they placed him in a basket and set it afloat on the Nile River. When the daughter of Pharaoh came to the river to bathe, she found Moses and took him into her home and raised him as her own. Hebrews 11:24 says, "By faith Moses, when he was come to years, refused to be called the son of Pharaoh's daughter."

Notice the word "refused." It is the Greek word *arneomai*, which means *to deny, to disown, to reject, to refuse, or to renounce*. It referred to *a person who disavowed, forsook, walked away from, or washed one's hands of another person or group of people.* Such denials were often accompanied by ridicule or persecution. The use of this word tells us that when Moses reached adulthood, he denied, disowned, and renounced that he was the son of Pharaoh's daughter. As a result, he was likely persecuted and ridiculed from walking away from such a position of prestige.

He Exchanged the Benefits of Royalty for Suffering With God's People

After forsaking and walking away from all his royal privileges, the Bible says Moses was found "choosing rather to suffer affliction with the people of God, than to enjoy the pleasures of sin for a season" (Hebrews 11:25). The word "choosing" in Greek is a form of the word *haireo*, which means *to choose* or *prefer*. It depicts *a personal choice or preference that sets one apart from others.* The phrase "suffer affliction with" is a translation of the Greek word *sunkakoucheo*, which depicts *joint suffering.* It means *to suffer bad things in partnership with others.* Moses chose to be affiliated with God's people who were suffering in slavery, and it set him apart in a very different category.

Isn't that amazing? Moses deliberately rejected the lavish living of Pharaoh's palace and chose to identify with God's people rather than "…enjoy the pleasures of sin for a season" (Hebrews 11:25). The word "enjoy" is the Greek word *apolausis*, and it describes *enjoyment* or *benefits.* The word "season" in Greek is *proskairos*, and it means *for a limited season; for a temporary season.* There were many benefits that came with being raised as the son of Pharaoh's daughter, but Moses could only enjoy them for a limited amount of time. By faith, he chose to walk away from all the temporary pleasures in exchange for the eternal benefits of following God.

He Esteemed the Reproach of Christ Greater Riches Than Egypt's Treasures

Continuing his description of the faith of Moses, the writer of Hebrews said that he chose to "[esteem] the reproach of Christ greater riches than the treasures in Egypt: for he had respect unto the recompence of the reward" (Hebrews 11:26).

The word "esteeming" in this verse is the Greek word *hegeomai*, and it means *to deem* or *to consider.* Moses *deemed* and *considered* the "…reproach of Christ greater riches than the treasures of Egypt…" (Hebrews 11:26). In Greek, the word "reproach" is *oneidismos*, and it describes *insults.* It is *language intended to injure, harm, hurt, or damage.* It denotes *words that damage one's reputation.* The use of this word *oneidismos* — translated here as "reproach" — tells us that when Moses walked away from the lap of luxury and chose to identify with the people of God, not only did he join them in suffering, he also subjected himself to a great deal of *verbal abuse.*

This brings us to the word "riches," which is the Greek word *plousios*, and it describes *wealth so great it cannot be tabulated.* It depicts *abundant or vast wealth*; *extreme riches*; *unlimited wealth*; *incredible abundance*; *opulence*; or *extravagant lavishness.* This word is a picture of *someone who possesses incredible abundance, extreme wealth, and enormous affluence.* Moses saw that in Christ, there are abundant riches beyond anything he had ever seen in the treasures of Egypt.

The word "treasures" here is the Greek word *thesauros*, which is a word describing *a treasure, a treasury, a treasure chamber, or a place of safekeeping where riches and fortunes are kept.* It presents the idea of *a special place designed as a repository for massive riches and wealth.* This word *thesauros* describes Egypt perfectly. It was so overflowing with riches that even the tombs of the previous pharaohs were filled with treasures. When Moses compared the physical treasures of Egypt with the supernatural riches God was offering, he determined that the riches of Christ were far greater than anything he had seen in the natural. These same riches are available to all believers in Christ — including you!

He Focused His Eyes on the Recompense of Reward That Would Come From God

Hebrews 11:26 concludes by saying, "…For he had respect unto the recompence of the reward." The word "respect" here is the Greek word *apoblepo*, which is a compound of the word *apo*, meaning *away*, and the word *blepo*, meaning *to look.* When these words are joined to form the word *apoblepo*, it means *to lift one's eyes to look away to see something else.* This means Moses had to take his eyes off of what he was walking away from in Egypt and fix them on what he was about to gain in God.

The Bible describes what he was about to gain as the "recompense of the reward." This phrase is a translation of the Greek word *misthapodosia* — the same word translated as "rewarder" in Hebrews 11:6. It is the word for *money, salary,* or *a payment that is due.* It denotes *one being reimbursed for an expense a person has paid out of his own pocket in order to get his job done.*

It was primarily used to denote *a payment, salary, or reward given for a job performed*, which means when you stay in your place of faith and do what God has called you to do, He will reimburse and reward you for all you've done. God pays those who stay in their place of faith.

Even though Moses had walked away from the extravagance of Egypt and all its treasures, when he lifted his eyes and looked into his future, he knew that God — the great Paymaster — was standing in front of him, and He was going to marvelously recompense him for his position of faith. And that is what God will do for you as well.

He Forsook Egypt and Endured in His Divine Calling

The Bible goes on to say, "By faith he [Moses] forsook Egypt, not fearing the wrath of the king: for he endured, as seeing him who is invisible" (Hebrews 11:27). The word "forsook" is the Greek word *kataleipo*, which means *to abandon and leave behind*. Moses *abandoned* Egypt and was not afraid of the king's "wrath." In Greek, the word "wrath" is *thumos*, and it portrays *a person who suddenly flares up and loses control; one who boils with anger and blows up, erupting in an ugly outburst that negatively affects other people*.

Instead of fearing Pharaoh's deep-seated anger, the Bible says that Moses "endured," which in Greek means *to be steadfast; to persevere;* or *continue undeterred*. Because Moses had lifted his eyes off of the treasures and pleasures of Egypt and fixed them on the full and complete recompense that was coming from God, the Great Paymaster, he was able to persevere and continue undeterred in his divine calling.

What else did Moses do through the unbendable, unbreakable, never-give-up kind of faith? Scripture says, "Through faith he kept the passover, and the sprinkling of blood, lest he that destroyed the firstborn should touch them. By faith they passed through the Red Sea as by dry land: which the Egyptians assaying to do were drowned" (Hebrews 11:28,29). In Greek, the phrase "passed through" is *diabaino*, which means, *walk through* or *step through*. Moses and the Israelites *walked through* the Red Sea "as by dry land," which literally means *as through dried up earth*. The power of God manifested in response to Moses' obedience.

Friend, Moses had to stay in his place of faith in order to please God and experience His power, and so do you. This means there may be times when you have to endure persecution, insults, and verbal abuse. Likewise, you will have to stand against the temptation to become cynical, doubtful, and unbelieving. But you can do it if you will align yourself with God's will and stay in faith. By staying active in your God-given assignment and tenaciously standing by — *hupostasis* — the promises He has made to you, you are in position for God — the Great Paymaster — to show up and reward you abundantly.

STUDY QUESTIONS

> Study to shew thyself approved unto God, a workman that needeth not to be ashamed, rightly dividing the word of truth.
> — 2 Timothy 2:15

1. When you think about Moses and all that you have learned about him, what do you admire most about his character? What new insights did you learn from this lesson about his life?
2. Take a moment to reread and reflect on Hebrews 11:24-26. In what ways are Moses' actions and attitude like that of Jesus? As you answer, consider Philippians 2:5-8 and Isaiah 53:2-5.

PRACTICAL APPLICATION

> But be ye doers of the word, and not hearers only, deceiving your own selves.
> — James 1:22

1. The Bible says that *by faith*, Moses purposely chose to walk away from all the privileges, prestige, and pleasures of being raised as the son of the daughter of Pharaoh. What is God asking you to walk away from? Are there certain worldly pleasures or relationships that the Holy Spirit is putting His finger on that you know you need to withdraw from? Get quiet in God's presence and meditate on Second Corinthians 6:14-18. What is He speaking to you in these moments?
2. From all that you've heard in this lesson on the life of Moses, what is most difficult to swallow? Is it walking away from certain pleasures and treasures? Is it choosing to suffer affliction that sometimes comes with following Christ? Or is it experiencing persecution and ridicule that often come from renouncing the world and its ways? Whatever you're struggling with, take time to tell God about it. He loves you

and wants to help you. If you will pour out your heart and invite Him in, He will strengthen your soul and spirit to submit to His will.

3. God promises you that if you will: "Roll your works upon the Lord [commit and trust them wholly to Him; He will cause your thoughts to become agreeable to His will, and] so shall your plans be established *and* succeed" (Proverbs 16:3 *AMPC*).

LESSON 9

TOPIC
Gideon, Barak, Sampson, Jephthae, David, Samuel, and Others

SCRIPTURES

1. **Hebrews 11:1-3,6** — Now faith is the substance of things hoped for, the evidence of things not seen. For by it the elders obtained a good report. Through faith we understand that the worlds were framed by the word of God, so that things which are seen were not made of things which do appear. ...But without faith it is impossible to please him: for he that cometh to God must believe that he is, and that he is a rewarder of them that diligently seek him.

2. **Hebrews 11:32-35** — And what shall I more say? for the time would fail me to tell of Gedeon, and of Barak, and of Samson, and of Jephthae; of David also, and Samuel, and of the prophets: Who through faith subdued kingdoms, wrought righteousness, obtained promises, stopped the mouths of lions. Quenched the violence of fire, escaped the edge of the sword, out of weakness were made strong, waxed valiant in fight, turned to flight the armies of the aliens. Women received their dead raised to life again: and others were tortured, not accepting deliverance; that they might obtain a better resurrection.

GREEK WORDS

1. "substance"— ὑπόστασις (*hupostasis*): a compound of ὑπό (*hupo*) and ἵστημι (*histimi*); the word ὑπό (*hupo*) means by and the word ἵστημι

(*histimi*) means to stand; literally, to stand by something; the attitude and actions of one who has determined to stand by something promised and refuses to budge from it; a fixed decision that one will be unmoving and he will stay or stand by a person, principle, promise, or territory

2. "worlds" — αἰῶνας (*aionas*): from αἰών (*aion*), an age or era; a specific time, age, or era within the past history of mankind; different periods of time

3. "framed" — καταρτίζω (*katartidzo*): to change, to mend, to adjust, or to alter the form or shape of an already existing thing; re-creating, reshaping, remolding, and altering of something that is already in existence; not so much the act of creation, but the act of transformation

4. "the word of God" — ῥήματι Θεοῦ (*rhemati Theou*): by a direct word from God

5. "without" — χωρίς (*choris*): without, as being outside of a specific place

6. "rewarder" — μισθαποδότης (*misthapodotes*): money, salary, or a payment that is due; can describe a recompense, reimbursement, settlement, or reparation; being reimbursed for an expense a person has paid out of his own pocket in order to get his job done; a full and complete recompense; in this case, the one who pays, rewards, or gives what one has coming to him; a paymaster

7. "diligently seek" — ἐκζητέω (*ekzeteo*): to zealously seek; one who seeks something so passionately that he exhausts all his power in his search for it; earnest effort; the idea of being hard-working, attentive, busy, constant, and persistent in one's devotion to what he or she is seeking

8. "subdued" — καταγωνίζομαι (*katagonidzomai*): from κατά (*kata*) and αγωνίζομαι (*agonidzomai*); the word κατά (*kata*) means down and αγωνίζομαι (*agonidzomai*) depicts agony; an intense conflict or contest; a struggle, fight great exertion, or effort; used to convey the ideas of anguish, pain, distress, and conflict, and it comes from the word ἀγών (*a-gon*) which pictured wrestlers in a wrestling match, with each wrestler struggling with all his might to overcome his opponent in an effort to hurl him to the ground in a fight to the finish

9. "wrought righteousness" — εἰργάσαντο δικαιοσύνην (*eirgasanto dikaiosunen*): carried out righteousness and justice

10. "obtained" — ἐπιτυγχάνω (*epitugchano*): obtain; fall upon; to light upon, as an army that pounces upon an enemy or who seizes treasures of war
11. "stopped" — φράσσω (*phrasso*): shut; close up; stop
12. "quenched" — σβέννυμι (*sbennumi*): to extinguish, smother, suppress, douse, put out, snuff out
13. "escaped" — φεύγω (*pheugo*): to flee, to take flight, to run away, to run as fast as possible, to escape; pictures one's feet flying as he runs from a situation
14. "out of weakness" — ἀπὸ ἀσθενείας (*apo astheneias*): from weakness; from a position of disability
15. "made strong" — δυναμόω (*dunamaoo*): empowered; made strong; made able; supernatural empowering
16. waxed "valiant" — ἰσχυρός (*ischuros*): a very strong man, such as a mighty man with great muscular capabilities; one who is able, mighty, and muscular; one with all the might and ability to overcome any foe or to accomplish any act needed; denotes might, power, strength, a great force or great ability
17. "fight" — πόλεμος (*polemos*): a full-scale, strategically fought war that is continued with unrelenting force until the enemy is incapacitated and victory is achieved; an organized and often prolonged military conflict designed to defeat an opponent
18. "turned to flight" — κλίνω (*klino*): literally, incline; to lay low; to put to bed
19. "others" — ἄλλοι (*alloi*): plural, others; indicating multiples
20. "tortured" — τυμπανίζω (*tumpanidzo*): to torture; refers to a wheel-shaped instrument of torture over which criminals were stretched as though they were skins and then horribly beaten with clubs
21. "deliverance" — ἀπολύτρωσις (*apolutrosis*): a release brought about by payment of ransom; redemption; deliverance

SYNOPSIS

The Winter Palace in Saint Petersburg, Russia, was once the headquarters of the Romanov family. As we have seen, a typical visit for foreign dignitaries and ambassadors began in the stunning Jordan Gallery and up the Jordan Staircase. Next, the Field Marshall Room, the Memorial Room of Peter the Great, the Coat of Arms Room, and then the Military Gallery of the War of 1812, which was a room commemorating Russia's victory over Napoleon.

The ultimate destination of each visiting diplomat was the Great Throne Room, which is officially called St. George's Hall. Historically, St. George was the patron saint of Russia, and an image of him slaying a dragon is depicted on the wall directly above the throne. The resplendent, neoclassical interior design of the Throne Room was simply breathtaking, and although it was lost in the great fire of 1837, it was virtually restored to its original splendor.

Today this great hall is surrounded by columns of magnificent white Carrara marble inlaid with streaks of blue marble. The ceiling is decorated with gold-gilded embellishments and features six massive gold-gilded chandeliers that sparkle as they refract light. With great precision, the intricate pattern on the ceiling is mirrored in the pattern of the parquet flooring. It is constructed of 16 precious woods including mahogany, which was used to accentuate the whiteness of the Carrara marble walls and columns.

St. George's Hall — the Great Throne Room — served as the Winter Palace's principle throne room since its inception and was the scene of most formal ceremonies of the Imperial Court. Sadly, during the 1917 revolution when the Bolsheviks entered into the palace, they ransacked everything and carried many of the important emblems of the Romanov Estate into the palace square where they were burned.

One of the things that was carried into the square and burned was the original throne from the Great Throne Room. The throne that is exhibited today is actually one from many years earlier, which was commissioned by Empress Ana. In any case, the Great Throne Room was a place for visiting dignitaries to come and see the tsar and his family. It was a place of great opulence and power commemorating the greatness of the Russian Empire.

Essentially, that is what "God's Hall of Faith" is in Hebrews 11. It is where He commemorates those who received a word from Him, got into alignment with Him, and did the impossible. Because of the great feats they accomplished by faith so long ago, they landed a place in "God's Hall of Faith." And God wants you to be in His Hall of Faith too!

The emphasis of this lesson:

Gideon, Barak, Sampson, Jephthae, David, Samuel, and the prophets are all included in "God's Hall of Faith." Their lives and the lives of countless others demonstrate that through faith we are supernaturally empowered to live righteously, act justly, fight valiantly, accomplish the impossible, and stay in faith even through times of intense struggle.

ACCORDING TO HEBREWS 11…

Faith Is a Fixed Decision

A major key to understanding God's Hall of Faith in Hebrews 11 is found in the first verse, which says, "Now faith is the substance of things hoped for, the evidence of things not seen" (Hebrews 11:1). The word "substance" in this verse is extremely important. It is the Greek word *hupostasis*, which is a compound of the word *hupo*, meaning *by*, and the word *histimi*, which means *to stand*. When these two words are compounded to form the word *hupostasis*, it literally means *to stand by something*. It depicts *the attitude and actions of one who has determined to stand by something promised and refuses to budge from it*. It is *a fixed decision that one will be unmoving and he will stay or stand by a person, principle, promise, or territory until he receives what has been promised*.

Faith Is Like a Bulldog on a Bone

As we have noted in each of the previous lessons, faith behaves like a bulldog that has found the bone of its dreams. Just as that dog wraps its jaws around its bone and refuses to let go, faith wraps its spiritual jaws around the promise of God and refuses to let go, regardless of how hard the devil fights or how other people try to take it away. A person in faith is going to stand by His promise and never let it go. Hence, you could translate the first part of Hebrews 11:1, "Faith is standing by things hoped for.…"

Faith Is an Act of Transformation

Hebrews 11:2 goes on to say, "For by it the elders obtained a good report." In other words, by the unbendable, unbreakable, never-give-up and never surrender type of faith, the "elders" — which in Greek refers to *the Old Testament heroes of faith* — obtained a good report.

Then in Hebrews 11:3 it says, "Through faith we understand that the worlds were framed by the word of God, so that things which are seen were not made of things which do appear." The word "worlds" here is the Greek word *aionas*, which is from the word *aion*, and it describes *an age* or *era*. It is *a specific time, age,* or *era within the past history of mankind.*

The word "framed" is the Greek word *katartidzo*, and it means *to change, to mend, to adjust, or to alter the form or shape of an already existing thing.* Thus, it indicates *re-creating, reshaping, remolding, and the altering of something that is already in existence.* It is not the act of creation, but the act of transformation.

Taking into account the meanings of these words, Hebrews 11:3 could be translated: "Through faith — through the unbendable, unbreakable, never-give-up, never surrender kind of faith — we understand that different time periods, different generations in past human history, have been modified, altered, and transformed by the word of God."

Faith Relentlessly Stands By God's Promises

What's interesting is that in the original Greek, the end of this verse actually says, "by a direct word from God," which is the theme emphasized throughout Hebrews 11. Each verse adds to the story of the elders of the Old Testament who received a word from God, and once they received that word, they spiritually wrapped their jaws around it. It was as if they said, "This is ours! We're going to latch hold of this word from God and relentlessly stand by it until we receive its manifestation."

And because these individuals came into alignment with God and agreed with His word, refusing to let go of it, they modified and changed their generation and their period of time. Their faith left the world in a different, better condition than it was when they first entered it.

Friend, that is the power *you* have. If God has spoken a word to you, wrap your jaws around it like a bulldog and never let it go! When the pressures of life and the attacks of the enemy assail you from every side and try to force you to release God's promises and walk away, make the choice to keep standing by what He said and never let it go.

Faith Is Staying in Your Divine Assignment and Diligently Seeking Him

Remember, the Bible says, "But without faith it is impossible to please him: for he that cometh to God must believe that he is, and that he is a rewarder of them that diligently seek him" (Hebrews 11:6). We have seen that the word "without" is the Greek word *choris*, and it means *without, as being outside of a specific place*. Hence, faith is a real *place* or *location*.

You are "without faith," or *outside* your place of faith, when you're *outside* of your God-given assignment and have walked away from what He promised you. And when you're outside of your place of faith, it is impossible for you to please God. Friend, your place of faith is being where God told you to be, doing what He told you to do, and standing by the promises He gave you until it becomes a reality.

What is the benefit of staying in your place of faith? The Bible says, "…[God] is a rewarder of them that diligently seek him" (Hebrews 11:6). The word "rewarder" in Greek describes *money, salary, or a payment that is due*. In this case, it describes God as the *Great Paymaster — one who pays, rewards, or gives what one has coming to him*.

The phrase "diligently seek," is the Greek word *ekzeteo*, and it means *to zealously seek*. It depicts *one who seeks something so passionately that he exhausts all his power in his search for it*. It describes *earnest effort* and carries the idea of *being hard-working, attentive, busy, constant, and persistent in one's devotion to what he or she is seeking*. When you stay in your place of faith and diligently seek God, the day is coming when He is going to show up as the Great Paymaster and reward you with a great recompense for your faith.

Faith Requires Great Effort and Great Energy

After the writer of Hebrews finished talking about Moses, he named several other Old Testament heroes who had received a word from God and stood by it faithfully until it came to pass. He said:

> And what shall I more say? for the time would fail me to tell of Gedeon, and of Barak, and of Samson, and of Jephthae; of David also, and Samuel, and of the prophets: Who through

faith subdued kingdoms, wrought righteousness, obtained promises, stopped the mouths of lions.
— Hebrews 11:32,33

Notice again, it says that through faith — through the unbendable, unbreakable, never-give-up kind of faith — they "subdued kingdoms." The word "subdued" is the Greek word *katagonidzomai*, which is a compound of the words *kata* and *agonidzomai*. The word *kata* means *down* and carries the idea of *domination*; and the word *agonidzomai* depicts *agony*. When these words are compounded to form the word *katagonidzomai*, it describes *an intense conflict or contest*; *a struggle, fight, great exertion, or effort*. This word was used to convey the ideas of *anguish, pain, distress, and conflict*, and it comes from the word *a-gon*, which pictured wrestlers in a wrestling match, with each wrestler struggling with all his might to overcome his opponent in an effort to hurl him to the ground in a fight to the finish.

The use of this word *katagonidzomai* — translated here as "subdued" — tells us that when these individuals were subduing kingdoms, it took great effort and great energy for them to hurl their enemies to the ground. This means that staying in your place of faith and accomplishing the assignment God has given you is not always easy. Sometimes it is a fight to the finish that involves pain and distress.

Faith Acts Righteously — Pouncing on God's Promises and Achieving the Impossible

In addition to subduing kingdoms, God's people of faith also "wrought righteousness," which in Greek means *they carried out deeds of righteousness and justice*. It was through faith that Samuel maintained God's standards of righteousness and justice in the land of Israel, acting as both a prophet and a judge to the nation.

They also "obtained promises." The word "obtained" is the Greek word *epitugchano*, which means *to fall upon* or *to light upon, as an army that pounces upon an enemy or who seizes treasures of war*. This is the same word used to describe a panther that leaps on a victim and overcomes him. The use of this word tells us that those who have received promises from God literally jumped on and pounced on them to take them as treasures of war.

Furthermore, the Bible says these heroes of faith "...stopped the mouths of lions" (Hebrews 11:33). The word "stopped" in Greek is the word *phrasso*, which means *to shut; close up; stop*. We know that by faith, Daniel prayed and shut the mouths of lions (*see* Daniel 6:22). Instead of being devoured, he was divinely kept by God's supernatural power.

The writer of Hebrews went on to say that *by faith*, the mighty saints of old "quenched the violence of fire..." (Hebrews 11:34) The word "quenched" is the Greek word *shennumi*, which means *to extinguish, smother, suppress, douse, put out,* or *snuff out*. Amazingly, a number of the Old Testament heroes smothered and snuffed out the violence of fires that were raging against them.

Still others "...escaped the edge of the sword..." (Hebrews 11:34). In Greek, the word "escaped" is *pheugo*, which means *to flee, to take flight, to run away, to run as fast as possible,* or *to escape*. It pictures one's feet flying as he runs from a situation. This lets us know that sometimes it takes faith to run away from a situation instead of staying in it and trying to fight it.

Through Faith, God's People Were Supernaturally Empowered To Fight

Hebrews 11:34 goes on to say that God's people of faith "...out of weakness were made strong...." The phrase "out of weakness" in Greek is *apo astheneias*, and it means *leaving weakness* or *from a position of disability*. The words "made strong" is the Greek word *dunamaoo*, which means *empowered; made strong;* or *made able*. It describes *a supernatural empowering*. Thus, there were Old Testament heroes of faith that stood by God's promises and *moved from a position of weakness to a position of supernatural empowerment*.

There were also men and women of faith who "...waxed valiant in fight, [and] turned to flight the armies of the aliens" (Hebrews 11:34). The words "waxed valiant" is a form of the Greek word *ischuros*, which pictures *a very strong man, such as a mighty man with great muscular capabilities*. It is *one who is able, mighty, and muscular; one with all the might and ability to overcome any foe or to accomplish any act needed*. Moreover, the word *ischuros* denotes *might, power, strength, a great force, or great ability*. When these Old Testament saints leaned on the Lord in faith, He *supernaturally empowered* them to stand toe-to-toe with their adversary so they waxed strong in fight.

This word "fight" is the Greek word *polemos*, and it describes *a full-scale, strategically fought war that is continued with unrelenting force until the enemy is incapacitated and victory is achieved*. It is *an organized and often prolonged military conflict designed to defeat an opponent*. The use of this word tells us that these believers were determined they would not stop standing in faith until their enemy was crushed — even if that meant they had to launch a full-scale strategically fought war. And it didn't matter how long they had to fight; they were going to wage war until they won their victory.

Not only did these faith-filled heroes wax valiant in fight, the Bible says they also "…turned to flight the armies of the aliens" (Hebrews 11:34). The phrase "turned to flight" is a translation of the Greek word *klino*, which means *to lay low* or *to put to bed*. A better translation of this part of the verse would be: *"They put to bed the armies of the aliens and knocked them flat on their backs."*

Through Faith Countless Believers Endured Torture

In Hebrews 11:35, the Bible goes on to say, "Women received their dead raised to life again…." Then the verse seems to abruptly change in the type of results that faith produces, saying, "…And others were tortured, not accepting deliverance; that they might obtain a better resurrection." To better understand what is being said here, let's take a look at the original Greek meaning of some of the key words in this verse.

First, it says, "…Others were tortured…." The word "others" is the Greek word *alloi*, which is plural, indicating *multiples*. Thus, there were great numbers who were "tortured." The word "tortured" is taken from the Greek word *tumpanidzo*, which means *to torture*. It specifically refers to *a wheel-shaped instrument of torture over which criminals were stretched as though they were skins and then horribly beaten with clubs*. This word very graphically depicts what some believers endured in order to stay in their place of faith.

It is vital to note that these individuals could have avoided being tortured by walking away from their confession of faith. But that is not what they chose to do. Instead, they tenaciously stood by (*hupostasis*) the word God had given them, refusing to quit and give up — even when faced with the consequences of being tortured.

In fact, the Bible says they chose to hold onto their faith and be tortured "…not accepting deliverance; that they might obtain a better resurrection" (Hebrews 11:35). The Greek word for "deliverance" here describes *a release brought about by payment of ransom*. It carries the idea of *redemption* and *deliverance*.

This tells us that there were people who were willing to pay a ransom or a bribe for these men and women of faith to get out of being tortured, but they rejected the payment being offered on their behalf. Essentially, they said, "We're not letting go of what God promised us! We're not going to surrender or leave our place of faith so that we might obtain a better resurrection."

Friend, these Old Testament saints chose to give everything they had to stand by their word from God, and that's what you have to do too. At times it will not be easy, and your assignment may be extremely difficult. But if you will stand by the word God gave you and say, "I'm not budging from my place of faith, nor am I going to let go of God's promise," He will release so much power to you and through you that everything around you will be changed!

STUDY QUESTIONS

Study to shew thyself approved unto God, a workman that needeth not to be ashamed, rightly dividing the word of truth.
— 2 Timothy 2:15

1. The Old Testament is filled with many amazing men and women who did great things for God, including people like Gideon, Deborah, Hannah, Samuel, and David. What Old Testament hero of faith do you most appreciate and admire? What is it about their character that excites and encourages you in your personal walk with God?
2. Throughout the gospels, the one thing that really blessed Jesus and made Him marvel was people's genuine faith. Take a moment to slowly read these examples of great faith. What stands out to you in the stories of these two people? What did each do that amazed Jesus?
   - The *Roman* Centurion (Matthew 8:5-13)
   - The *Canaanite* Woman (Matthew 15:21-28)

3. Is there a person in your life — present or past — that you would consider to be a modern-day hero of faith? Who is it? How is their life displaying unbendable, unbreakable, never-give-up faith?

PRACTICAL APPLICATION

> But be ye doers of the word, and not hearers only, deceiving your own selves.
> —James 1:22

1. The Bible says that through faith certain people "…escaped the edge of the sword…" (Hebrews 11:34), which means they *took flight and ran away as fast as possible.* This lets us know that sometimes the behavior of faith is *to run away* from a situation instead of staying in it and trying to fight. Have you ever experienced such a situation? Are you dealing with something now that you need faith to run from? (Consider First Corinthians 6:18; Second Timothy 2:22; and Proverbs 5:8 as you answer.)
2. Through faith, God's people "…out of weakness were made strong…" (Hebrews 11:34). This means they moved from a position of weakness into a position of supernatural empowerment. Are you facing a situation right now that has drained you of strength? Pray and ask the Holy Spirit to empower you with supernatural ability to stand by God's promises (*hupostasis*) until you see His victory manifested. If you are at a loss of words, pray in the Spirit! He knows exactly what to pray when you don't know what to say (*see* Romans 8:26,27; Jude 20).

LESSON 10

TOPIC

Unnamed Giants of Faith

SCRIPTURES

1. **Hebrews 11:1-3,6** — Now faith is the substance of things hoped for, the evidence of things not seen. For by it the elders obtained a good report. Through faith we understand that the worlds were framed by the word of God, so that things which are seen were not made of

things which do appear. ...But without faith it is impossible to please him: for he that cometh to God must believe that he is, and that he is a rewarder of them that diligently seek him.
2. Hebrews 11:36-40 — And others had trial of cruel mockings and scourgings, yea, moreover of bonds and imprisonment: they were stoned, they were sawn asunder, were tempted, were slain with the sword: they wandered about in sheepskins and goatskins; being destitute, afflicted, tormented; (of whom the world was not worthy:) they wandered in deserts, and in mountains, and in dens and caves of the earth. And these all, having obtained a good report through faith, received not the promise: God having provided some better thing for us, that they without us should not be made perfect.

GREEK WORDS

1. "substance" — ὑπόστασις (*hupostasis*): a compound of ὑπό (*hupo*) and ἵστημι (*histimi*); the word ὑπό (*hupo*) means by and the word ἵστημι (*histimi*) means to stand; literally, to stand by something; the attitude and actions of one who has determined to stand by something promised and refuses to budge from it; a fixed decision that one will be unmoving and he will stay or stand by a person, principle, promise, or territory

2. "worlds" — αἰῶνας (*aionas*): from αἰών (*aion*), an age or era; a specific time, age, or era within the past history of mankind; different periods of time

3. "framed" — καταρτίζω (*katartidzo*): to change, to mend, to adjust, or to alter the form or shape of an already existing thing; re-creating, reshaping, remolding, and altering of something that is already in existence; not so much the act of creation, but the act of transformation

4. "the word of God" — ῥήματι Θεοῦ (*rhemati Theou*): by a direct word from God

5. "without" — χωρίς (*choris*): without, as being outside of a specific place

6. "rewarder" — μισθαποδότης (*misthapodotes*): money, salary, or a payment that is due; can describe a recompense, reimbursement, settlement, or reparation; being reimbursed for an expense a person has paid out of his own pocket in order to get his job done; a full and

complete recompense; in this case, the one who pays, rewards, or gives what one has coming to him; a paymaster

7. "diligently seek" — ἐκζητέω (*ekzeteo*): to zealously seek; one who seeks something so passionately that he exhausts all his power in his search for it; earnest effort; the idea of being hard-working, attentive, busy, constant, and persistent in one's devotion to what he or she is seeking

8. "others" — ἕτεροι (*heteroi*): others of a different kind; New Testament believers

9. "trial" — πεῖρα (*peira*): an intense trial

10. "cruel mockings" — ἐμπαιγμός (*empaigmos*): to play a game; often used for playing a game with children or for amusing a crowd by impersonating someone in a silly and exaggerated way; might be used in a game of charades when someone intends to comically portray someone or even to make fun of, ridicule, or mock someone

11. "scourgings" — μάστιξ (*mastix*): borrowed from the world of torture; denoted the act of recurrently beating a prisoner or victim; once a person's wounds had mended, the torturers often brought him back to the whipping post, where he was struck again and again; although usually not serious enough to kill, such beatings kept a victim in constant pain and misery; torment and abuse, a scourge that caused great suffering and prolonged anguish

12. "imprisonments" — φυλακή (*phulake*): a Roman prison, one of the most dreadful places in the Roman world

13. "stoned" — λιθάζω (*lithadzo*): to stone; to overwhelm or bury with stones; to assail with stones with the intention to kill

14. "sawn asunder" — πρίζω (*pridzo*): to saw; to cut into two pieces; pictures the horrible practice of sawing in half

15. "tempted" — πειράζω (*peiradzo*): to put to the test; depicts a test to expose the truth about the quality of a substance; an intense examination or questioning; an interrogation

16. "slain" (by the sword) — φόνος (*phonos*): to slaughter; to massacre; butchery and carnage

17. "wandered" — περιέρχομαι (*perierchomai*): to wander; to roam; to move around

18. "sheepskins" and "goatskins" — could refer to Nero's brutal killing of believers; the Roman historian Tacitus recorded that Nero had Christians covered in wild beast skins and torn to death by dogs
19. "destitute" — ὑστερέω (*hustereo*): to be lacking; depleted; impoverished; suffering physical need
20. "afflicted" — θλίβω (*thlibo*): to be pressured; compressed; suffocated
21. "tormented" — κακουχέω (*kakoucheo*): to oppress; to torment; to maltreat
22. "world" — κόσμος (*kosmos*): world system; society
23. "wandering" — πλανάω (*planao*): to wander; roaming
24. "deserts" — ἔρημος (*eremos*): pictures a deserted place; a remote spot; a place out of the way; somewhere off the beaten track; an obscure site
25. "mountains" — ὄρος (*oros*): a mountain or a hill
26. "dens" — ὀπή (*ope*): holes in the earth, usually in remote locations
27. "caves" — σπήλαιον (*spelaion*): a den; caves; caverns; hiding places
28. "obtained a good report" — μαρτυρέω (*martureo*): a testimony in a court of law; one who is commended by his testimony
29. "received not" — κομίζω (*komidzo*): receive; to convey to someone else; to receive what is due; to receive what one has coming to him
30. "provided" — προβλέπομαι (*problepomai*): to see beforehand; to see in advance
31. "better" — κρείττων (*kreitton*): comparatively much better, much stronger, more excellent
32. "without us" — χωρίς (*choris*): without, as being outside of a specific place; apart and distinct from us
33. "perfect" — τελειόω (*teleioo*): to reach the end-stage; to reach the final phase; to reach the final conclusion; to reach the aim

SYNOPSIS

In each of the previous lessons, we have explored the magnificent Winter Palace, which is located on the Neva River in Saint Petersburg, Russia. It is a huge complex consisting of three floors and a full basement, encompassing about 2,511,000 square feet. The interiors of this palace, together with the adjoining Hermitage Museum, are the equivalent of about 12 football fields — all under one roof. In fact, if you take all the hallways and line them up in a straight line, it totals 15 miles of hallway!

The interiors of the Winter Palace were simply marvelous beyond description. The walls were covered with exquisite marble along with embellishments of gold, silver, and precious stones. Rare statues of every kind from the ancient world and huge chandeliers dazzled each dignitary as they made their way through each room and finally arrived in the Great Throne Room where they would meet and greet the tsar and his family.

From the moment visitors entered the palace until the time they left, they were surrounded by famous faces, places, names, and events all commemorating the great deeds in the history of the Russian Empire. The entire palace was designed to remind guests of the distinguished individuals in the past who had done mighty deeds.

That is what Hebrews 11 is all about. It is "God's Hall of Faith," and He has written it to remind us of the ordinary people who did extraordinary things. They received a word from God, obeyed what He said, and it changed their generation. That is what will happen to you if you will hear and receive God's word and then do what He says. You, too, will end up in God's ever-expanding Hall of Faith.

The emphasis of this lesson:

Along with the Old Testament heroes of faith, there are New Testament heroes mentioned in God's Hall of Faith. They endured cruel mockings, scourgings, and imprisonment and were made to wander in deserts and mountains. Through every form of suffering imaginable, these believers obtained a good report and opened the way of faith for us today.

A Final Review of Our Anchor Verses

Faith Is Standing By Things Hoped For

The Bible says, "Now faith is the substance of things hoped for, the evidence of things not seen" (Hebrews 11:1). The word "substance" in Greek is the word *hupostasis*, which is a compound of the words *hupo* and *histimi*. The word *hupo* means *by*, and the word *histimi* means *to stand*. When these two words are compounded to form *hupostasis*, it literally means *to stand by something*. It is *the attitude and actions of one who has determined to stand by something promised and who refuses to budge from it*. It denotes *a fixed decision that one will be unmoving and he will stay or stand by a person, principle, promise, or territory that has been promised until he receives the full manifestation of it*.

The word "substance" — the Greek word *hupostasis* — describes how faith *behaves*, which is actually a lot like a bulldog that has found the bone of its dreams. No matter how hard you try to pull that bone away, once that dog has wrapped its jaws around it, he's going to stand by his bone and never let it go. In the same way, when you're in faith, you tenaciously stand by what God has said He would do for your marriage, your family, your business, your church, and your community. Like a bulldog clutching its bone, you continue to hold tightly to God's promises and never let them go.

When the going gets tough, and life's circumstances begin to cave in on top of you, the temptation to walk away from God's promises drastically increases. That is what was happening to the First-Century Hebrew believers and why the writer of Hebrews wrote to them and said, "Cast not away therefore your confidence, which hath great recompence of reward" (Hebrews 10:35). To "cast away your confidence" is to throw away your bold, confident confession of faith. It is to abandon your God-given assignment and walk away from the promises God gave you. The Bible describes this condition as to be "without faith."

Inside of Your Place of Faith, You Can Please God

Hebrews 11:6 says, "But without faith it is impossible to please [God]...." We learned that the word "without" is the Greek word *choris*, and it means *without, as being outside of a specific place*. Thus, the phrase "without faith" does not describe an absence of faith — it describes faith as a *location*. For instance, you can be *inside* your house or *outside* your house, but you can't be in both places at the same time. This word *choris* — translated here as "without" — depicts a person who has chosen to be *outside* of faith.

So *faith is a place*, and your place of faith is God's assignment for you — it is being where God told you to be, doing what He told you to do, believing what He said to believe and not moving from it. Consequently, to walk away from the promises God gave you and leave the place He assigned to you is to be "without (outside of) faith" — a position where it is impossible to please God.

If You Will Diligently Seek Him, He Will Reward You

Hebrews 11:6 goes on to say, "...For he that cometh to God must believe that he is, and that he is a rewarder of them that diligently seek him." The word "rewarder" is the Greek word *misthapodotes*, and it describes *money, salary, or a payment that is due.* It can also describe *a recompense, reimbursement, settlement, or reparation.* It depicts *a person being reimbursed for an expense he has paid out of his own pocket in order to get his job done, a full and complete recompense.* In this verse, it denotes *the one who pays, rewards, or gives what one has coming to him*; *a paymaster.*

This means if you'll stay in your assignment and continue to stand on the promise (or promises) God gave you and refuse to let go, the day is coming when God — the Great Paymaster — is going to show up and reward you with a great recompense for your faith. But this reward only comes to those who "diligently seek Him."

In Greek, the phrase "diligently seek" is the word *ekzeteo*, and it means *to zealously seek.* It depicts *one who seeks something so passionately that he exhausts all his power in his search for it.* This word denotes *earnest effort* and carries the idea of *being hard-working, attentive, busy, constant, and persistent in one's devotion to what he or she is seeking.*

The use of the word *ekzeteo* — translated here as "diligently seek" — indicates that staying in your place of faith requires a great deal of hard work. You have to be attentive, active, and committed to staying in your assignment and standing by the promises God gave you. If you pray and ask God for His strength, He will empower you with His Holy Spirit to stay in your place of faith.

By Faith, New Testament Believers Endured Many Forms of Suffering

So far, we've looked at the elders of the Old Testament and heard the writer of Hebrews talk about prophets, kings, and common people who received a word from God and stood by it until it came to pass. These were all ordinary people who did extraordinary things that transformed their generation and the world itself. Then when we come to Hebrews 11:36, the Bible says, "And others had trial of cruel mockings and scourgings, yea, moreover of bonds and imprisonment."

Notice the word "others." It is the Greek word *heteroi*, which means *others of a different kind.* Up until this point the writer of Hebrews has focused on the lives of Old Testament heroes, but now he shifts his attention to New Testament believers and begins to describe the price they paid to relentlessly stand by — *hupostasis* — the promises of God in faith.

Cruel Mockings, Scourgings, and Imprisonment

First, the Bible says, "And others had trial of cruel mockings and scourgings…" (Hebrews 11:36). The word "trial" is the Greek word *peira*, and it describes *an intense trial*. The phrase "cruel mockings" is a translation of the Greek word *empaigmos*, which means *to play a game*. This word was often used for *playing a game with children or for amusing a crowd by impersonating someone in a silly and exaggerated way*. It might be used in a game of charades when someone intends to comically portray someone or even to make fun of, ridicule, or mock someone. The use of this word lets us know that New Testament believers were often mocked and made fun of. They became a laughingstock to unbelievers and were humiliated regularly.

The word "scourgings" in Greek is the word *mastix*, which is borrowed from the world of torture. It denoted *the act of recurrently beating a prisoner or victim*. Once a person's wounds had mended, the torturers often brought him back to the whipping post, where he was struck again and again. Although the blows were usually not serious enough to kill, such beatings kept a victim in constant pain and misery. This word depicts *a scourge that caused great suffering and prolonged anguish, torment, and abuse*.

First-Century Christians also endured "bonds and imprisonment." The word "bonds" describes *one that is completely bound*. And the word "imprisonment" is a translation of the Greek word *phulake*, which is the word for *a Roman prison*, one of the most dreadful places in the Roman world. Many believers were locked up in Roman prisons for their faith in Christ.

Stoned, Sawn Asunder, Tempted, and Slain

The writer of Hebrews continues to describe the plight of New Testament believers saying, "They were stoned, they were sawn asunder, were tempted, were slain with the sword…" (Hebrews 11:37).

The word "stoned" is the Greek word *lithadzo*, which means *to stone*; *to overwhelm or bury with stones*; or *to assail with stones with the intention to kill*. The Scripture also says some believers were "sawn asunder," which is a translation of the Greek word *pridzo*, meaning *to saw* or *to cut into two pieces*. It pictures *the horrible practice of sawing an individual in half*.

Moreover, the Bible says believers were "tempted," which is the Greek word *peiradzo*, which means *to put to the test*. It depicts *a test to expose the truth about the quality of a substance*; *an intense examination or questioning*;

an interrogation. This word was used to describe the process of testing coins to determine if they were authentic or counterfeit. These believers had made a bold confession of faith, and the devil was testing them to see just how genuine their faith was. Would they hold onto the word they had received from God, or would they cast away their confidence to escape the pressure the enemy was bringing? If he could get them to abandon the promises of God, then their faith was not what they claimed it to be.

What else did First Century believers experience? The Bible says they were "...slain with the sword..." (Hebrews 11:37). The word "slain" is the Greek word *phonos*, which means *to slaughter* or *to massacre*. It describes *the barbaric butchery and carnage* that some followers of Christ went through at the hands of ungodly men.

They Wandered About in Sheepskins and Goatskins

The writer of Hebrews went on to say that there were also Christians who "...wandered about in sheepskins and goatskins; being destitute, afflicted, tormented" (Hebrews 11:37). The word "wandered" here is the Greek word *perierchomai*, which means *to wander; to roam*; or *to move around*. The reference to "sheepskins" and "goatskins" could refer to Nero's brutal killing of believers. The Roman historian Tacitus recorded that Nero had Christians covered in wild beast skins and torn to death by dogs.

The Bible also says a number of believers were "destitute," which is a translation of the Greek word *hustereo*, and it means *to be lacking; depleted; impoverished*; or *suffering physical need*. Still others were "afflicted and tormented." In Greek, the word "afflicted" is the word *thlibo*, and it means *to be pressured, compressed*, or *suffocated*. And the word "tormented" is the Greek word *kakoucheo*, which means *to oppress, to torment*, or *to maltreat*.

First-Century believers experienced all these forms of abuse and torture, and yet they did not let go of the promises God had given them. Instead, they continued to stand by the word they had received, and they brought God great glory.

They Wandered in Deserts, Mountains, Dens, and Caves

In Hebrews 11:38, the writer said that these believers "(of whom the world was not worthy:) they wandered in deserts, and in mountains, and in dens and caves of the earth." In this verse, the word "world" is a form of the Greek word *kosmos*, and it describes *the world system* or *society during that age.* The world at that time was not worthy of the caliber of people these Christians were.

Yet these followers of Christ ended up wandering everywhere. The word "wandering" here is the Greek word *planao*, which means *to wander* or *to roam*. The first place these persecuted believers ended up was in "deserts," which is the Greek word *eremos*, and it pictures *a deserted place; a remote spot; a place out of the way;* or *somewhere off the beaten track; an obscure site.* They also wandered in "mountains" — from the Greek word *oros*, which describes *a mountain or a hill.*

More than likely, it was in these deserts and mountains that believers found "dens" and "caves" in which to dwell. The word "dens" is the Greek word *ope*, which literally describes *holes in the earth, usually in remote locations;* and the word "caves" is the Greek word *spelaion*, which describes *a den; caves; caverns;* or *hiding places.* As castaways from society, many Christians learned to live their lives in seclusion.

These Believers Obtained a Good Report

When we come to Hebrews 11:39, the Bible says, "And these all, having obtained a good report through faith, received not the promise." The phrase "obtained a good report" is the Greek word *martureo*, which describes *a testimony in a court of law; one who is commended by his testimony.* It is a form of the Greek word *martus*, which is from where we get the word *martyr.* This word was predominantly used to describe either *a witness who was summoned to testify in a court of law* or *the evidence or proof presented in a legal case.*

In New Testament times, to be a witness — *martus* — meant one could be placed in jeopardy, even of losing one's life. They faced the risk that other people who did not appreciate their testimony would persecute or afflict them for telling the truth. Nevertheless, a faithful witness was willing to tell the truth regardless of the ramifications.

In this case, these believers "obtained a good report" because they refused to let go of the promise God had given them. They gave their testimony of Jesus and refused to recant their confession of faith. And the Bible says they "…received not the promise" (Hebrews 11:39). The phrase "received not" is a form of the Greek word *komidzo*, which means *to receive* or *to receive what one has coming to him.* In this case, it means they did *not* receive what was due or what they had coming to them because God had something far better in mind.

God Had Much Bigger and Better Blessings in Mind

The writer of Hebrews wraps up the eleventh chapter saying, "God having provided some better thing for us, that they without us should not be made perfect" (Hebrews 11:40). The word "provided" here is the Greek word *problepomai*, which means *to see beforehand* or *to see in advance*. The word "better" is the Greek word *kreitton*, which means *comparatively much better, much stronger, more excellent*. This means God was able to look very far into the future and see a better, stronger, and more excellent reward for His people.

Verse 40 goes on to say, "...that they without us should not be made perfect" (Hebrews 11:40). The phrase "without us" is again the Greek word *choris*, meaning *without, as being outside of a specific place*. It can also mean *apart and distinct from us*. And the word "perfect" is the Greek word *teleioo*, which means *to reach the end-stage; to reach the final phase; to reach the final conclusion*; or *to reach the aim*.

The *Amplified Classic* version of Hebrews 11:40 makes what is being said here very clear: "Because God had us in mind *and* had something better *and* greater in view for us, so that they [these heroes and heroines of faith] should not come to perfection apart from us [before we could join them]."

The bottom line is, these men and women of God stayed in faith, despite the life-threatening conditions they endured. And while they, themselves, did not see the manifestation of the promise they were holding on to, we are standing in the manifestation of what they were believing God for.

Friend, you have to stay in faith. Even if you don't see the manifestation of God's promise now, the next generation will. Just like Isaac, Jacob, and Joseph, you have to shift your faith to believe God's promise is going to come to pass on your children and grandchildren. And when life tries to take it from you, you have to set your face like flint and say, "God's promise is mine! I've wrapped my spiritual jaws around it, and I will never let it go — even if I have to shift my faith to believe it's going to happen in the lives of my kids or my grandkids. I'm never going to release the word that God gave me. I'm going to stay in my place of faith." Friend, you can do it because "...[You] can do all things through Christ which strengtheneth [you]!" (Philippians 4:13).

STUDY QUESTIONS

> Study to shew thyself approved unto God, a workman that needeth not to be ashamed, rightly dividing the word of truth.
> — 2 Timothy 2:15

1. As you read through Hebrews 11:36-40 and heard about the many different forms of suffering that Early Christians endured, how does it change the way you see the hardships you are going through?
2. One of the greatest guarantees God has given us — especially when we go through very difficult situations — is that He is always with us and will never leave us. Take time to really chew on this powerful promise:

   "…**For He [God] Himself has said, I will not in any way fail you nor give you up nor leave you without support. [I will] not, [I will] not, [I will] not in any degree leave you helpless nor forsake nor let [you] down (relax My hold on you)! [Assuredly not!] So we take comfort and are encouraged and confidently and boldly say, The Lord is my Helper; I will not be seized with alarm [I will not fear or dread or be terrified]. What can man do to me?"**
   — Hebrews 13:5,6 (*AMPC*)

   How does this promise encourage and embolden you in your faith?
3. Another powerful promise from God to wrap your spiritual jaws around is found in **First Corinthians 10:13**. Look up this verse in a few different Bible versions and write out the one that really comes alive and encourages your heart.

PRACTICAL APPLICATION

> But be ye doers of the word, and not hearers only, deceiving your own selves.
> — James 1:22

1. Have you or someone you know ever been mocked or ridiculed for taking a stand for righteousness? If so, describe what took place. How has this situation shaped and strengthened your faith in God?
2. The Bible says that New Testament believers were "tempted," which is the Greek word *peiradzo*, and it means *to put to the test*. It depicts *a test*

or an intense examination to expose the truth about the quality of something. Have you ever been tested in this way? If you have, explain what happened. What did the intense investigation show you about *yourself* that you hadn't seen before? What did it show you about *God* and how did it draw you closer to Him?

3. The Bible says, "Because God had us in mind *and* had something better *and* greater in view for us, so that they [these heroes and heroines of faith] should not come to perfection apart from us [before we could join them]" (Hebrews 11:40 *AMPC*). Who can you think of that is no longer alive whose tenacious faith helped you connect more deeply in your relationship with God? Who are you impacting with your life of faith, and how are you selflessly making an eternal difference in their lives?

4. As you complete this study on "God's Hall of Faith," what do you feel is the most important thing that you learned that you don't want to forget — and that you want to share with others?

Notes

Notes

www.ingramcontent.com/pod-product-compliance
Lightning Source LLC
Chambersburg PA
CBHW061451040426
42450CB00007B/1313